HISTORIC HIGHWAYS OF AMERICA

VOLUME 12

HISTORIC HIGHWAYS OF AMERICA
VOLUME 12

Pioneer Roads and Experiences of Travelers

(Volume II)

BY

ARCHER BUTLER HULBERT

With Maps

THE ARTHUR H. CLARK COMPANY
CLEVELAND, OHIO
1904

CONTENTS

ILLUSTRATIONS

PREFACE

THIS volume is devoted to two great lines of pioneer movement, one through northern Virginia and the other through central New York. In the former case the Old Northwestern Turnpike is the key to the situation, and in the latter the famous Genesee Road, running westward from Utica, was of momentous importance.

A chapter is given to the Northwestern Turnpike, showing the movement which demanded a highway, and the legislative history which created it. Then follow two chapters of travelers' experiences in the region covered. One of these is given to the *Journal of Thomas Wallcutt* (1790) through northern Virginia and central Pennsylvania. Another chapter presents no less vivid descriptions from quite unknown travelers on the Virginian roads.

The Genesee Road is presented in chap-

ter four as a legislative creation; the whole
history of this famous avenue would be
practically a history of central New York.
To give the more vivid impression of per-
sonal experience a chapter is devoted to a
portion of Thomas Bigelow's *Tour to Niagara Falls 1805* over the Genesee Road in
its earliest years, when the beautiful cities
which now lie like a string of precious
gems across this route were just springing
into existence. For a chapter on the important " Catskill Turnpike," which gives
much information of road-building in central New York, we are indebted to Francis
Whiting Halsey's *The Old New York
Frontier*.

The final chapter of the volume includes
a number of selections from the spicy,
brilliant descriptions of pioneer traveling
in America which Dickens left in his
American Notes, and a few pages describing
an early journey on Indian trails in Missouri from Charles Augustus Murray's
Travels in North America.

A. B. H.

MARIETTA, OHIO, January 26, 1904.

Pioneer Roads and
Experiences of Travelers
(Volume II)

CHAPTER I

THE OLD NORTHWESTERN TURNPIKE

WE have treated of three historic highways in this series of monographs which found a way through the Appalachian uplift into the Mississippi Basin — Braddock's, Forbes's, and Boone's roads and their successors. There were other means of access into that region. One, of which particular mention is to be made in this volume, dodged the mountains and ran around to the lakes by way of the Mohawk River and the Genesee country. Various minor routes passed westward from the heads of the Susquehanna — one of them becoming famous as a railway route, but none becoming celebrated as roadways. From central and southern Virginia, routes, likewise to be followed by trunk railway lines, led onward toward the Mississippi Basin, but none, save only Boone's track, became of prime importance.

But while scanning carefully this mountain barrier, which for so long a period held back civilization on the Atlantic seaboard, there is found another route that was historic and deserves mention as influencing the westward movement of America. It was that roadway so well known three-fourths of a century ago as the Old Northwestern Turnpike, leading from Winchester, Virginia, to the Ohio River at Parkersburg, Virginia, now West Virginia, at the mouth of the Little Kanawha.

The earliest history of this route is of far more interest than importance, for the subject takes us back once more to Washington's early exploits and we feel again the fever of his wide dreams of internal communications which should make the Virginia waterways the inlet and outlet of all the trade of the rising West. It has been elsewhere outlined how the Cumberland Road was the actual resultant of Washington's hopes and plans. But it is in place in a sketch of the Old Northwestern Turnpike to state that Washington's actual plan of making the Potomac River all that the

Erie Canal and the Cumberland Road became was never even faintly realized. His great object was attained — but not by means of his partisan plans.

It is very difficult to catch the exact old-time spirit of rivalry which existed among the American colonies and which always meant jealousy and sometimes bloodshed. In the fight between Virginia officers in Forbes's army in 1758 over the building of a new road through Pennsylvania to Fort Duquesne, instead of following Braddock's old road, is an historic example of this intense rivalry. A noted example, more easily explained, was the conflict and perennial quarrel between the Connecticut and Pennsylvania pioneers within the western extremity of the former colony's technical boundaries. That Washington was a Virginian is made very plain in a thousand instances in his life; and many times it is emphasized in such a way as must seem odd to all modern Americans. At a stroke of a pen he shows himself to be the broadest of Americans in his classic Letter to Benjamin Harrison, 1784; in the next sentence he is urging Virginia to look

well to her laurels lest New York, through
the Hudson and Mohawk, and Pennsylvania, through the Susquehanna and
Juniata, do what Virginia ought to do
through her Potomac.

The powerful appeal made in this letter
was the result of a journey of Washington's
in the West which has not received all the
attention from historians it perhaps deserves. This was a tour made in 1784 in
the tangled mountainous region between
the heads of the branches of the Potomac
and those of the Monongahela.[1] Starting
on his journey September 1, Washington
intended visiting his western lands and returning home by way of the Great Kanawha
and New Rivers, in order to view the con-
nection which could be made there between
the James and Great Kanawha Valleys.
Indian hostilities, however, made it unwise
for him to proceed even to the Great
Kanawha, and the month was spent in
northwestern Virginia.

On the second, Washington reached
Leesburg, and on the third, Berkeley;
here, at his brother's (Colonel Charles

[1] Washington's *Journal* Sept. 2nd to Oct. 4th, 1784.

Washington's) he met a number of persons
including General Morgan. " . . one
object of my journey being," his *Journal*
reads, " to obtain information of the nearest and best communication between the
Eastern & Western Waters; & to facilitate
as much as in me lay the Inland Navigation
of the Potomack; I conversed a good deal
with Gen[l]. Morgan on this subject, who
said, a plan was in contemplation to extend a Road from Winchester to the
Western Waters, to avoid if possible an
interference with any other State." It is
to be observed that this was a polite way of
saying that the road in contemplation must
be wholly in Virginia, which was the only
state to be " interfered " with or be bene-
fited. " But I could not discover," Washington adds, " that Either himself, or
others, were able to point it out with pre-
cision. He [Morgan] seemed to have no
doubt but that the Counties of Freder[k].,
Berkeley & Hampshire would contribute
freely towards the extension of the Navigation of Potomack; as well as towards
opening a Road from East to West."

It should be observed that the only route

across the mountains from northwestern
Virginia to the Ohio River was Braddock's
Road; for this road Washington was a
champion in 1758, as against the central
route Forbes built straight west from
Bedford to Fort Duquesne.[2] Then, however, Braddock's Road, and even Fort
Duquesne, was supposed to lie in Virginia.
But when the Pennsylvania boundaries
were fully outlined it was found that Braddock's Road lay in Pennsylvania. Washington now was seeking a new route to the
West which would lie wholly in Virginia.
The problem, historically, presents several
interesting points which cannot be ex-
panded here. Suffice it to say that Washington was the valiant champion of Braddock's Road until he found it lay wholly
in Maryland and Pennsylvania.

Gaining no satisfaction from his friends
at Berkeley, Washington pushed on to one
Captain Stroad's, out fourteen odd miles
on the road to Bath. "I held much conversation with him," the traveler records
of his visit at Stroad's, "the result   .   .
was,—that there are two Glades which go

[2]*Historic Highways of America*, vol. v, ch. 3.

under the denomination of the Great
glades — one, on the Waters of Yohiogany,
the other on those of Cheat River; &
distinguished by the name of the Sandy
Creek Glades.— that the Road to the first
goes by the head of Patterson's Creek [3]—
that from the acc[ts]. he has had of it, it is
rough; the distance he knows not.— that
there is a way to the Sandy Creek Glades
from the great crossing of Yohiogany
(or Braddocks Road) [Smithfield, Pennsyl-
vania] & a very good one; .   ." At
the town of Bath Washington met one
Colonel Bruce who had traversed the
country between the North Branch (as
that tributary of the Potomac was widely
known) and the Monongahela. " From
Col[o]. Bruce .   . I was informed that
he had travelled from the North Branch of
Potomack to the Waters of Yaughiogany,
and Monongahela — that the Potom[k]. where
it may be made Navigable — for instance
where McCulloughs path crosses it, 40

[3] This creek rises in Hardy County, Virginia, and flows
northeastward through Hampshire County, entering the
North Branch of the Potomac River about eight miles
southeast of Cumberland, Maryland.

Miles above the old fort [Cumberland], is
but about 6 Miles to a pretty large branch
of the Yohiogany .   . — that the Waters
of Sandy Creek which is a branch of cheat
River, which is a branch of Monongahela,
interlocks with these; and the Country
between, flat — that he thinks (in order to
ev^d. [evade] passing through the State of
Pennsylvania) this would be an eligible
Road using the ten Miles C^k. with a portage
to the Navigable Waters of the little
Kanhawa; .   ."

This was the basis of Washington's plan
of internal communication from Potomac;
he now pressed forward to find if it were
possible to connect the Youghiogheny and
North Branch of the Potomac, the Youghiogheny and Monongahela, and the Monongahela and Little Kanawha.   Of course the
plan was impossible, but the patient man
floundered on through the foothills and
mountains over what was approximately
the course mentioned, the "McCullough's
Path" and Sandy Creek route from the Potomac to the Monongahela.   In his explorations he found and traversed one of the
earliest routes westward through this

broken country immediately south of the
well known resorts, Oakland and Deer
Park, on the Baltimore and Ohio Railway.
This was the "McCullough's" Path already
mentioned. Having ascended the Monongahela River from near Brownsville, Pennsylvania, Washington, on September 24,
arrived at a surveyor's office (the home
of one Pierpoint) eight miles southward
along the dividing ridge between the
Monongahela and Cheat Rivers.[4] On the
twenty-fifth—after a meeting with various
inhabitants of the vicinity—he went plung-
ing eastward toward the North Branch of
the Potomac " along the New Road [which
intersected Braddock's Road east of Winding Ridge] to Sandy Creek; & thence by
McCullochs path to Logstons [on the North
Branch of the Potomac] and accordingly
set of [off] before Sunrise. Within 3 Miles
I came to the river Cheat ab^t. 7 Miles
from its Mouth — .   . The Road from
Morgan Town or Monongahela C^t. House,
is said to be good to this ferry [Ice's] —
distance abt. 6 Miles[5] .   . from the

[4] Union Township, Monongalia County, West Virginia.
[5] Oliphant's Iron Furnace, Union Township?

ferry the Laurel Hill [6] is assended . .
along the top of it the Road continues. . . After crossing this hill the
road is very good to the ford of Sandy
Creek at one James Spurgeons,[7] . .
ab^t. 15 Miles from Ice's ferry. At the
crossing of this Creek McCullocks path,
which owes its origen to Buffaloes, being
no other than their tracks from one lick
to another & consequently crooked & not
well chosen, strikes off from the New
Road. . . From Spurgeon's to one
Lemons, which is a little to the right of
McCullochs path, is reckoned 9 Miles, and
the way not bad; but from Lemons to the
entrance of the Yohiogany glades [8] which is
estimated 9 Miles more thro' a deep rich
Soil · . . and what is called the briery
Mountain.[9] . . At the entrance of

[6] The mountainous boundary line between Monongalia
and Preston Counties.

[7] Bruceton's Mills, Grant Township, Preston County,
West Virginia?

[8] Southwestern corner of Maryland, some twenty
miles north of Oakland.

[9] Briery Mountain runs northeast through the eastern
edge of Preston County, bounding Dunkard Bottom on
the east as Cheat River bounds it on the west.

the above glades I lodged this night, with
no other shelter or cover than my cloak. &
was unlucky enough to have a heavy shower
of Rain. . . 26th. . . passing
along a small path . . loaded with
Water . . we had an uncomfortable
travel to one Charles friends [10] about 10
Miles. . . A Mile before I came to
Friends, I crossed the great Branch of
Yohiogany. . . Friend . . is
a great Hunter. . . From Friends
I passed by a spring (distant 3 Miles) called
Archy's from a Man of that name — crossed

[10] The Friends were the earliest pioneers of Garrett
County, John Friend coming in 1760 bringing six sons
among whom was this Charles. The sons scattered
about through the valley of the Youghiogheny, Charles
settling near the mouth of Sang Run, which cuts
through Winding Ridge Mountain and joins the
Youghiogheny about fifteen miles due north from Oakland. Washington, moving eastward on McCulloch's
Path probably passed through this gap in Winding
Ridge. A present-day road runs parallel with Winding
Ridge from Friendsville (named from this pioneer
family) southward to near Altamont, which route
seems to have been that pursued by McCulloch's Path.
See Scharf's *History of Western Maryland*, vol. ii, p.
1518; *Atlas of Maryland* (Baltimore, 1873), pp. 47–48;
War Atlas 1861–65, *House Miscellaneous Documents*,
vol. iv, part 2, No. 261, 52d Cong. 1st Sess. 1891–92,
Plate cxxxvi.

the backbone [11] & descended into Ryans
glade.[12]—Thence by Tho[s]. Logston's . . to
the foot of the backbone, about 5 Miles . .
across the Ridge to Ryans glade one mile
and half .   . —to Joseph Logstons 1½
Miles .   . —to the N°. Branch at
McCullochs path 2 Miles [13] — infamous
road — and to Tho[s]. Logstons 4 more. . .
27th. I left M[r]. Logston's .   . —at ten
Miles I had .   . gained the summit
of the Alligany Mountain [14] and began to
desend it where it is very steep and bad to
the Waters of Pattersons Creek .   .
along the heads of these [tributaries], &
crossing the Main [Patterson's] Creek &

[11] Great Back Bone Mountain, Garrett County, Maryland, on which, at Altamont, the Baltimore and Ohio
Railway reaches its highest altitude. It was about here
that Washington now crossed it, probably on the
watershed between Youghiogheny and Potomac waters
west of Altamont.

[12] Ryan's Glade No. 10, Garrett County.

[13] This point is pretty definitely determined in the
Journal. We are told that the mouth of Stony River
(now Stony Creek) was four miles below McCulloch's
crossing. This would locate the latter near the present
site of Fort Pendleton, Garrett County, Maryland, the
point where the old Northwestern Turnpike crossed the
North Branch.

[14] Greeland Gap, Grant County, West Virginia.

Mountain bearing the same name [15] (on the top of which at one Snails I dined)   I came to Col°. Abrah^m. Hites at Fort pleasant on the South Branch [16] about 35 Miles from Logstons a little before the Suns setting. My intention, when I set out from Logstons, was to take the Road to Rumney [Romney] by one Parkers but learning from my guide (Joseph Logston) when I came to the parting paths at the foot of the Alligany [17] (ab^t. 12 Miles) that it was very little further to go by Fort pleasant, I resolved to take that Rout .   . to get information.   .   ."

This extract from Washington's journal gives us the most complete information obtainable of a region of country concern-

[15] Knobby Mountain.

[16] Near Moorefield, Hardy County, West Virginia.

[17] Mt. Storm, Grant County.   The Old Northwestern Turnpike bears northeast from here to Claysville, Burlington and Romney.   Washington's route was southwest along the line of the present road to Moorefield. Evidently the buffalo trace bore southwest on the watershed between Stony River and Abraham's Creek — White's *West Virginia Atlas* (1873), p. 26.   Bradley's *Map of United States* (1804) shows a road from Morgantown to Romney; also a "Western Fort" at the crossing-place of the Youghiogheny.

ing which it is difficult to secure even
present-day information. The drift of the
pioneer tide had been on north and south
lines here; the first-comers into these
mountains wandered up the Monongahela
and Youghiogheny Rivers and their tribu-
taries. Even as early as the Old French
War a few bold companies of men had
sifted into the dark valleys of the Cheat
and Youghiogheny.[18] That it was a difficult country to reach is proved by the fact
that certain early adventurers in this region
were deserters from Fort Pitt. They were
safe here! A similar movement up the
two branches of the Potomac had created a
number of settlements there — far up where
the waters ran clear and swift amid the
mountain fogs. But there had been less
communication on east and west lines. It
is easy to assume that McCulloch's path
was the most important route across the
ragged ridges, from one glade and valley

[18] Dunkard's Bottom, in Portland Township, Preston
County, West Virginia, was settled about 1755 by Dr.
Thomas Eckarly and brothers who traversed the old
path to Fort Pleasant on South Branch.—Thwaites's
edition of Withers's *Chronicles of Border Warfare*
(1895), pp. 75–76.

to another. It is entirely probable that
the New Road, to which Washington
refers, was built for some distance on the
buffalo trace which (though the earlier
route) branched from the New Road. An
old path ran eastward from Dunkard's Bottom of which Washington says: "   .   .
being   .   .   discouraged   .   .   from
attempting to return [to the Potomac] by
the way of Dunkars Bottom, as the path it
is said is very blind & exceedingly grown
up with briers, I resolved to try the other
Rout, along the New Road   .   ." as
quoted on page 21. The growth of such
towns as Cumberland and Morgantown
had made a demand for more northerly
routes. The whole road-building idea in
these parts in the last quarter of the eight-
eenth century was to connect the towns
that were then springing into existence,
especially Morgantown and Clarksburg
with Cumberland. Washington's dream of
a connected waterway was, of course,
hopelessly chimerical, and after him no
one pushed the subject of a highway of
any kind between the East and the West
through Virginia. Washington's own

plans materialized in the Potomac Navigation Company, and his highway, that
should be a strong link in the chain of
Federal Union between the improved Potomac and the Ohio, became the Cumberland Road; and it ran just where he did
not care to see it — through Maryland and
Pennsylvania. Yet it accomplished his
first high purpose of welding the Union
together, and was a fruit of that patriotic
letter to Governor Harrison written a few
days after Washington pushed his way
through the wet paths of the Cheat and
Youghiogheny Valleys in 1784.

These first routes across the mountains
south of the Cumberland Road — in Virginia — were, as noted, largely those of
wild beasts. "It has been observed before," wrote Washington in recapitulation,
"to what fortuitous circumstances the paths
of this Country owe their being, & how
much the ways may be better chosen by a
proper investigation of it; . ." In
many instances the new roads built here-
abouts in later days were shorter than the
earlier courses; however it remains true
here, as elsewhere, that the strategic geog-

raphical positions were found by the buffalo
and Indian, and white men have followed
them there unwaveringly with turnpike
and railway.

When Washington crossed the North
Branch of the Potomac on the 26th of October, 1784 at "McCullochs crossing," he
was on the track of what should be, a
generation later, the Virginian highway
across the Appalachian system into the
Ohio Basin. Oddly enough Virginia had
done everything, it may truthfully be said,
toward building Braddock's Road to the
Ohio in 1755, and, in 1758, had done as
much as any colony toward building
Forbes's Road. All told, Virginia had
accomplished more in the way of road-
building into the old Central West by 1760
than all other colonies put together. Yet,
as it turned out, not one inch of either of
these great thoroughfares lay in Virginia
territory when independence was secured
and the individual states began their struggle for existence in those "critical" after-
hours. These buffalo paths through her
western mountains were her only routes;
they coursed through what was largely an

uninhabited region, and which remains
such today. Yet it was inevitable that a
way should be hewn here through Virginia
to the Ohio; the call from the West, the
hosts of pioneers, the need of a state way
of communication, all these and more,
made it sure that a Virginia Turnpike
should cross the mountains.

Before that day arrived the Cumberland
Road was proposed, built, and completed,
not only to the Ohio River, but almost to
the western boundary of the state of Ohio;
its famous successor of another generation,
the Baltimore and Ohio Railway, was undertaken in 1825. These movements stirred
northern Virginians to action and on the
twenty-seventh of February, 1827, the
General Assembly passed an act " to incor-
porate the North-western Road Company."

Sections 1, 3, 4, and 5 of this Act are as
follows:

" 1. *Be it enacted by the General Assembly
of Virginia*, That books shall be opened at
the town of Winchester, in Frederick
county, under the direction of Josiah Lock-
hart, William Wood, George S. Lane,
Abraham Miller, and Charles Brent, or any

two of them; at Romney, in Hampshire
county, under the direction of William
Naylor, William Donaldson, John M'Dow-
ell, Robert Sherrard, and Thomas Slane,
or any two of them; at Moorfield, in Hardy
county, under the direction of Isaac Van
Meter, Daniel M'Neil, Benjamin Fawcett,
Samuel M'Machen, and John G. Harness,
or any two of them; at Beverly, in Ran-
dolph county, under the direction of Eli
Butcher, Squire Bosworth, Jonas Crane,
Andrew Crawford, and William Cooper, or
any two of them; at Kingwood, in Preston
county, under the direction of William
Sigler, William Johnson, William Price,
Charles Byrne, and Thomas Brown, or any
two of them; at Pruntytown, in Harrison
county, under the direction of Abraham
Smith, Frederick Burdett, Thomas Gethrop,
Cornelius Reynolds, and Stephen Neill, or
any two of them; at Clarksburg, in Harrison
county, under the direction of John L.
Sehon, John Sommerville, John Webster,
Jacob Stealy, and Phineas Chapin, or any
two of them; and at Parkersburg, in Wood
county, under the direction of Jonas Beason,
Joseph Tomlinson, Tillinghast Cook, James

H. Neal, and Abraham Samuels, or any
two of them, for purpose of receiving subscriptions to a capital stock of seventy-five
thousand dollars, in shares of twenty dollars, to be appropriated to the making of a
road from Winchester to some proper place
on the Ohio river, between the mouths
of   Muskingum,   and   Little   Kanawha
rivers, according to the provisions of this
act.   .   .

" 3.   The proceedings of the first general meeting of the stockholders, shall be
preserved with subsequent proceedings of
the company, all of which shall be entered
of record in well bound books to be kept
for that purpose: And from and after the
first appointment of directors, the said re-
sponsible subscribers, their heirs and as-
signs, shall be, and they are hereby declared
to be, a body politic and corporate, by the
name of ' The North western Road Company;'   .   .

" 4.   It shall be the duty of the Principal Engineer of the State, as soon as exist-
ing engagements will permit, to prescribe
such plans or schemes for making the
whole road, or the several parts or sections

thereof, as he shall think best calculated
to further its most proper and speedy completion, and to locate and graduate the
same, or part or parts thereof, from time to
time, make estimates of the probable cost
of making each five miles, (or any shorter
sections,) so located and graduated, and to
make report thereof to the Board of Public
Works at such time or times as shall be
convenient.

" 5. The said president and directors
shall, from time to time, make all contracts
necessary for the completion of the said
road, and shall require from subscribers
equal advances and payments on their
shares, and they shall have power to com-
pel payments by the sale of delinquent
shares, in such a manner as shall be prescribed by their by-laws, and transfer the
same to purchasers: *Provided*, That if any
subscriber shall at any time be a contractor
for making any part of the said road, or in
any other manner become a creditor of the
company, he shall be entitled to a proper
set-off in the payment of his stock, or any
requisition made thereon.   .   ." [19]

[19] *Laws of Virginia* (1826–1827), pp. 85–87.

A mistake which doomed these plans to failure was in arbitrarily outlining a road by way of the important towns without due consideration of the nature of the country between them. The mountains were not to be thus mocked; even the buffalo had not found an east and west path here easily. As noted, the towns where subscriptions were opened were Winchester, Romney, Moorefield, Beverly, Kingwood, Prunty-town,.Clarksburg, and Parkersburg. When the engineers got through Hampshire County by way of Mill Creek Gap in Mill Creek Mountain and on into Preston County, insurmountable obstacles were encountered and it was reported that the road would never reach Kingwood. From that moment the North-western Road Company stock began to languish; only the intervention of the state saved the enterprise. However, in 1831, a new and very remarkable act was passed by the Virginia Assembly organizing a road company that stands unique in a road-building age. This was " An act to provide for the construction of a turnpike road from Winchester to some point on the Ohio river." The governor

was made president of the company and he
with the treasurer, attorney-general, and
second auditor constituted the board of
directors. The 1st, 2d, and 4th sections of
this interesting law are as follows:

" 1. *Be it enacted by the general assembly*,
That the governor, treasurer, attorney
general, and second auditor of the commonwealth for the time being, and their
successors, are hereby constituted a body
politic and corporate, under the denomination of ' The President and Directors of the
North-Western Turnpike Road,' with
power to sue and be sued, plead and be
impleaded, and to hold lands and tene-
ments, goods and chattels, and the same to
sell, dispose of, or improve, in trust for the
commonwealth, for the purposes herein-
after mentioned. And three of the
said commissioners shall constitute a board
for the transaction of such business as is
hereby entrusted to them; of which board,
when present, the governor shall be president: And they shall have power to appoint a clerk from without their own body,
and make such distribution of their duties
among themselves respectively, and such

rules and regulations .   . as to them
may seem necessary.   .   .

" 2. *Be it further enacted*, That the said
president and directors of the North-Western turnpike road be, and they are hereby
empowered as soon as may be necessary for
the purposes herein declared, to borrow on
the credit of the state, a sum or sums of
money not exceeding one hundred and
twenty-five thousand dollars, and at a rate
of interest not exceeding six per centum
per annum.   .   .

" 4. *Be it further enacted*, That the said
president and directors, out of the money
hereby authorized to be borrowed, shall
cause to be constructed a road from the
town of Winchester, in the county of Frederick, to some point on the Ohio river, to
be selected by the principal engineer.
And for the purpose aforesaid, the principal engineer, as soon as may be after the
passage of this act, shall proceed to lay out
and locate the said road from the points
above designated. He shall graduate the
said road in such manner that the acclivity
or declivity thereof shall in no case exceed
five degrees. The width of the said road

may be varied, so that it shall not exceed eighteen feet, nor be less than twelve feet. Through level ground it shall be raised in the middle one-twenty-fourth part of its breadth, but in passing along declivities it may be flat. Bridges, side ditches, gutters, and an artificial bed of stone or gravel, shall be dispensed with, except in such instances as the said principal engineer may deem them necessary.   .   ."[20]

Other sections stipulated that the state had the right to survey any and all routes the engineers desired to examine, and that persons suffering by loss of land or otherwise could, if proper application was made within one year, secure justice in the superior or county courts; that the company appoint a superintendent who should have in charge the letting of contracts after such were approved by the company; that, as each stretch of twenty miles was completed, toll gates could be erected thereon, where usual tolls could be collected by the company's agents, the total sum collected to be paid into the state treasury; that the

[20]*Laws of Virginia* (1831), pp. 153–158; *Journal of the Senate   .   . of Virginia* (1830–31), p. 165.

company had the right to erect bridges, or in case a ferry was in operation, to make the ferryman keep his banks and boats in good condition; that the company make annual reports to the State Board of Public Works; and that the road be forever a public highway.

The roadway was now soon built. Not dependent upon the stock that might be taken in the larger towns, the road made peace with the mountains and was built through the southern part of Preston County in 1832, leaving Kingwood some miles to the north. Evansville was located in 1833, and owes its rise to the great road. The route of the road is through Hampshire, Mineral, Grant, Garrett, Preston, Taylor, Harrison, Doddridge, Ritchie, and Wood Counties, all West Virginia save Garrett which is in Maryland. Important as the route became to the rough, beautiful country which it crossed, it never became of national importance. Being started so late in the century, the Baltimore and Ohio Railway, which was completed to Cumberland in 1845, stopped in large part the busy scenes of the Old Northwestern Turnpike.

Yet to the historic inquirer the old turnpike, so long forgotten by the outside
world, lies where it was built; and can
fairly be said to be a monument of the last
of those stirring days when Virginia
planned to hold the West in fee. Hundreds of residents along this road recall
the old days with intense delight. True,
the vast amount of money spent on the
Cumberland Road was not spent on its less
renowned rival to the south, but the Cumberland Road was given over to the states
through which it ran; and, in many instances, was so neglected that it was as
poor a road as some of its less pretentious
rivals. A great deal of business of a national character was done on the Northwestern Turnpike. Parkersburg became
one of the important entrepôts in the Ohio
Valley; as early as 1796, we shall soon see,
a pioneer traversing the country through
which the Northwestern Turnpike's prede-
cessor coursed, speaks of an awakening in
the Monongahela Valley that cannot be
considered less than marvelous. Taking
it through the years, few roads have remained of such constant benefit to the

territory into which they ran, and today
you will be told that no railway has bene-
fited that mountainous district so much as
this great thoroughfare.

But in a larger sense than any merely
local one, Virginia counted on the Northwestern Turnpike to bind the state and
connect its eastern metropolis with the
great Ohio Valley. Virginia had given
up, on demand, her great county of Kentucky when the wisdom of that movement
was plain; at the call of the Nation, she
had surrendered the title her soldiers had
given her to Illinois and the beautifully
fertile Scioto Valley in Ohio. But after
these great cessions she did not lose the
rich Monongahela country. It had been
explored by her adventurers, settled by
her pioneers — and Virginia held dear to
her heart her possessions along the upper
Ohio. In the days when the Northwestern
Turnpike was created by legislative act,
canals were not an assured success, and
railways were only being dreamed of.
And the promoters of canals and railways
were considered insane when they hinted
that the mountains could be conquered by

leys. We walked this day about twenty-
three or twenty-four miles, and slept near
the forty-fourth or forty-fifth mile tree.

" Wednesday, 10 March, 1790. Weather
raw and moist. To-day we crossed several
of the large creeks and waters that fall into
the Ohio. This occasioned a loss of much
time, waiting for the horse to come over
for each one, which he did as regularly as
a man would. The country much the
same, but rather better to-day, except that
a great deal of the road runs along through
the streams, and down the streams such a
length with the many bridges that will be
wanted, that it will be a vast expense,
besides the risk and damage of being carried away every year by the floods. We
had so much trouble in crossing these
streams that at last we forded on foot.
One of the largest in particular, after we
had rode it several times, we waded it four
or five times almost knee-deep, and after
that a number of times on logs, or otherwise, without going in water. Two of the
streams, I doubt not, we crossed as often as
twenty times each. We walked this day
about fifteen miles.

" Thursday, 11 March, 1790. With much fatigue and pain in my left leg, we walked about fifteen miles to-day. They all walked better than I, and had got to Carpenter's and had done their dinner about two o'clock when I arrived. They appear to be good farmers and good livers, have a good house, and seem very clever people. Mr. C. is gone down the country. They have been a frontier here for fifteen years, and have several times been obliged to move away. I got a dish of coffee and meat for dinner, and paid ninepence each, for the doctor and me. We set off, and crossed the west branch of the Monongahela over to Clarksburgh. The doctor paid his own ferriage. We went to Major Robinson's, and had tea and meat, &c., for supper. I paid ninepence each, for the doctor and me. Weather dull and unpleasant, as yesterday.

" Friday, 12 March, 1790. Weather good and pleasant to-day. We set off before sunrise and got a little out of our road into the Morgantown road, but soon got right again. We breakfasted at Webb's mill, a good house and clever folks. Had coffee, meat, &c.; paid sixpence each, for me and the doctor. Lodged at Wickware's, who says he is a Yankee, but is a very disagreeable man for any country, rough and ugly, and he is very dear. I paid one shilling apiece for the doctor's and my supper, upon some tea made of mountain birch, perhaps black birch, stewed pumpkin, and sodden meat. Appetite supplies all deficiencies.

"Saturday, 13 March, 1790. Beautiful weather all day. Set off not so early this morning as yesterday. The doctor paid his ferriage himself. Mr. Moore, a traveller toward his home in Dunker's Bottom, Fayette County, Pennsylvania, [?] set out with us. He seems a very mild, good-natured, obliging old gentleman, and lent me his horse to ride about two miles, while he drove his pair of steers on foot. The doctor and I being both excessively fatigued, he with a pain in his knee, and mine in my left leg, but shifting about, were unable to keep up with our company, and fell much behind them. Met Mr. Carpenter on his return home. He appears to be a very clever man. When we had come to Field's, I found Mr. Dodge had left his horse for us to ride, and to help us along, which we

could not have done without. We got a
dish of tea without milk, some dried
smoked meat and hominy for dinner; and
from about three o'clock to nine at night,
got to Ramsay's. Seven miles of our way
were through a new blazed path where
they propose to cut a new road. We got
out of this in good season, at sundown or
before dark, into the wagon road, and
forded Cheat River on our horses. Tea,
meat, &c., for supper. Old Simpson and
Horton, a constable, had a terrible scuffle
here this evening.

"Lord's Day, 14 March, 1790. Mr.
Dodge is hurrying to go away again. I
tell him I must rest to-day. I have not
written anything worth mention in my
journal since I set out, until to-day, and so
must do it from memory. I want to shave
a beard seven days old, and change a shirt
about a fortnight dirty; and my fatigue
makes rest absolutely necessary. So take
my rest this day, whether he has a mind to
go or stay with us. Eat very hearty of
hominy or boiled corn with milk for breakfast, and boiled smoked beef and pork for
dinner, with turnips. After dinner shaved

and shirted me, which took till near night,
it being a dark house, without a bit of window, as indeed there is scarce a house on
this road that has any.

"Monday, 15 March, 1790. Waited and
got some tea for breakfast, before we set
out. Settled with Ramsay, and paid him
9*d*. per meal, for five meals, and half-pint
whiskey 6*d*. The whole came to eight
shillings. Weather very pleasant most of
the day. We walked to Brien's about half-
past six o'clock, which they call twenty-
four miles. We eat a little fried salt pork
and bit of venison at Friends',[27] and then
crossed the great Youghiogeny. About
two miles further on, we crossed the little
ditto at Boyles's. . . We walked
about or near an hour after dark, and were
very agreeably surprised to find ourselves
at Brien's instead of Stackpole's, which is
four miles further than we expected. Eat
a bit of Indian bread, and the woman gave
us each about half a pint of milk to drink,
which was all our supper.

[27] Near Friendsville, Maryland — named in honor of
the old pioneer family; see note 10, *ante;* cf. Corey's
map of Virginia in his *American Atlas* (1805), 3d edition; also Samuel Lewis's *Map of Virginia* (1794).

"Tuesday, 16 March, 1790. We were
up this morning, and away about or before
sunrise, and ascended the backbone of the
Alleghany, and got breakfast at Williams's.
I cannot keep up with my company. It
took me till dark to get to Davis's. Messers.
Dodge and Proctor had gone on before us
about three miles to Dawson's. We got
some bread and butter and milk for supper,
and drank a quart of cider. Mr. Davis was
originally from Ashford, county of Wind-
ham, Connecticut; has been many years
settled in this country; has married twice,
and got many children. His cider in a
brown mug seemed more like home than
any thing I have met with.

"Wednesday, 17 March. We were up
this morning before day, and were set off
before it was cleverly light. Got to Dawson's, three miles, where Messers. D. & P.
lodged, and got some tea for breakfast, and
set off in good season, the doctor and I
falling behind. As it is very miry, fatiguing
walking, and rainy, which makes extremely
painful walking in the clay and mud, we
could not keep up with D. We stopped
about a mile and a half from the Methodist

meeting near the cross roads at Cressops,
and four from Cumberland, and got some
fried meat and eggs, milk, butter, &c.,
for dinner, which was a half pistareen
each. After dinner the doctor and I walked
into Cumberland village about three o'clock,
and put up at Herman Stitcher's or Stid-
ger's. We called for two mugs of cider,
and got tea, bread and butter, and a boiled
leg of fresh young pork for supper. The
upper part of the county of Washington
has lately been made a separate county,
and called Alleghany, as it extends over
part of that mountain, and reaches to the
extreme boundary of Maryland. The
courts, it is expected, will be fixed and
held at this place, Cumberland, which will
probably increase its growth, as it thrives
pretty fast already. We supped and breakfasted here; paid 2s. for each, the doctor
and me. Pleasant fine weather this day.
My feet exceedingly sore, aching, throbbing, and beating. I cannot walk up with
my company.

" Thursday, 18 March. Paid Mr. Dodge
6s. advance. A very fine day. We stayed
and got breakfast at Stitcher's, and walked

from about eight o'clock to twelve, to Old
Town, and dined at Jacob's, and then
walked to Dakins's to lodge, where we got
a dish of Indian or some other home coffee,
with a fry of chicken and other meat for
supper.   This is the first meal I have paid
a shilling L. M. for.   The country very
much broken and hilly, sharp high ridges,
and a great deal of pine.   About   .   .
miles from Old Town, the north and south
branches of the Potomac join.   We walked
twenty-five miles to-day.

" Friday, 19 March, 1790.   Very fine
weather again to-day.   We walked twenty-
four miles to McFarren's in Hancock, and
arrived there, sun about half an hour high.
McFarren says this town has been settled
about ten or twelve years, and is called for
the man who laid it out or owned it, and
not after Governor Hancock.   It is a small
but growing place of about twenty or thirty
houses, near the bank of the Potomac,
thirty-five miles below Old Town, and five
below Fort Cumberland; twenty-four above
Williamsport, and ninety-five above George-
town.   We slept at McFarren's, a so-so
house.   He insisted on our sleeping in

beds, and would not permit sleeping on the floors. We all put our feet in soak in warm water this evening. It was recommended to us by somebody on the road, and I think they feel the better for it.

"Saturday, 20 March. A very fine day again. We have had remarkably fine weather on this journey hitherto. But two days we had any rain, and then but little. We stayed and got breakfast at McFarren's, and set out about eight o'clock, and walked about twenty-one miles this day to Thompson's, about half a mile from Buchanan's in the Cove Gap in the North Mountain. My feet do not feel quite so bad this day, as they have some days. I expect they are growing stronger and fitter for walking every day, though it has cost me a great deal of pain, throbbing, beating, and aching to bring them to it. It seems the warm water last night did me some good.

"Lord's Day, 21 March, 1790. Up and away before sunrise, and walked to breakfast to McCracken's. He has been an officer in the continental army. I find it will not do for me to try any longer to keep

up with my company, and as they propose
going through Reading, and we through
Philadelphia, we must part to-night or to-
morrow.   I conclude to try another seven
miles, and if I cannot keep up, we part at
Semple's, the next stage. They got to Semple's before me, and waited for me.   I conclude to stay and dine here, and part with
Messrs. Proctor and Dodge.   I am so dirty;
my beard the ninth day old, and my shirt
the time worn, that I cannot with any
decency or comfort put off the cleaning any
longer.   I again overhauled the letters, as
I had for security and care taken all into
my saddle-bags.   I sorted them and gave
Mr. Dodge his, with what lay more direct
in his way to deliver, and took some from
him for Boston and my route.

"I paid Mr. Dodge three shillings more
in addition to six shillings I had paid him
before at the Widow Carrel's, according to
our agreement at twelve shillings to Philadelphia; and as we had gone together and
he had carried our packs three hundred
miles (wanting two), it was near the matter.   He supposed I should do right to give
him a shilling more.   I told him as I had

agreed with him at the rate of fifty pounds, when they did not weigh above thirty-five, and at the rate of going up to Pitt instead of returning, which is but half price, I thought it was a generous price, and paid him accordingly as by agreement. We wished each other a good journey, and Mr. Proctor, the doctor, and I drank a cup of cider together. When we had got cleaned, a wagoner came along very luckily, and dined with us, and going our way, we put our packs in his wagon, and rode some to help. We gave him a quarter of a dollar for this half day and tomorrow. We got to Carlisle in the evening and put up with Adam at Lutz's.

" This Carlisle is said to be extremely bad in wet weather. It probably is nearly & quite as bad as Pittsburg, Marietta, Albany. I went to Lutz's because Adam puts up there, he being of his nation, but it is a miserable house, and Adam says he is sorry he carried us there. The victuals are good, but they are dirty, rough, impolite. We supped on bread and milk, and Lutz would insist on our sleeping in a bed and not on the floor; so we did so.

" Tuesday, 23 March, 1790. A pleasant
day and the roads very much dried, so
that the travelling is now comfortable.
We dined at Callender's in more fashion
than since I left home. Adam stopped at
Simpson's so long that it was dark when we
got over the river to Chambers's, where we
stopped another half hour. Set off about
seven o'clock, and got to Foot's about
eleven. All abed, but Adam got us a bit
of bread and butter, and made us a fire in
the stove, and we lay on the floor.

" Wednesday, 24 March, 1790. Old Foot
is a crabbed. . . He has been scold-
ing and swearing at Adam all this morning
about something that I cannot understand.
It has rained last night, and the roads are
again intolerable. Adam says he cannot
go again until his father says the word,
and that may not be this two or three days.
But we cannot go and carry our packs on
our backs now, the roads are so bad, and
we should gain nothing to walk, but spend
our strength to little or no purpose. We
must wait for a wagon to go along our
way, and join it, or wait for the roads to
grow better.

" Carried our dirty things to wash; two shirts, two pairs stockings, and one handkerchief for me; two shirts, two pair stockings, and one pair trowsers for the doctor. Went to several places to look for shoes for the doctor. He could not fit himself at the shoemakers, and bought a pair in a store for 8s. 4d. Pennsylvania, or 6s. 8d. our currency. He went to Henry Moore's, the sign of the two Highlanders. I drank a quart of beer and dined. Old Foot is a supervisor, and is gone to Harrisburg to-day, to settle some of his business.

" Thursday, 25 March, 1790. The sun rises and shines out so bright to-day that I am in hopes the roads will be better, at least, when we go. Old Foot could not finish his business yesterday, and is gone again to-day. He is uncertain when he shall send Adam forward to Philadelphia, perhaps not until Monday. It will not do for us to stay, if we can somehow get along sooner. Time hangs heavy on our hands, but we do what we can to kill it. The doctor and I went down to Moore's and dined together, which was a shilling L. M. apiece. We then came back to Foot's and drank a pint of cider-royal together. The house is for the most part of the day filled with Germans, who talk much, but we cannot understand them. We have coffee and toast, or meat for breakfast, and mush and milk for supper. Our time is spent in the most irksome manner possible; eating and drinking, and sleeping and yawning, and attending to the conversation of these Dutch. In the evening the house is crowded with the neighbors, &c., and for the .   .   Old Foot says, and Adam too, that he will not go till Monday. This is very discouraging.

" Friday, 26 March, 1790. A very dull prospect to-day. It rained very hard in the night, and continues to rain this morning. No wagons are passing, and none coming that we can hear of. We have no prospect now but to stay and go with Adam on Monday. We stay at home to-day and murder our time. We read McFingal, or Ballads, or whatever we can pick up. We had coffee and toast and fresh fried veal for breakfast, and ate heartily, and so we eat no dinner. The doctor goes out and buys us 8*d*. worth of cakes, and we get a half-pint of whiskey, which makes us a little less sad. In comes a man to inquire news, &c., of two men from Muskingum. He had heard Thompson's report, which had made so much noise and disquiet all through the country. He had three Harrisburg papers with him, which give us a little relief in our dull and unwelcome situation. At dark there come in two men with a wagon and want lodging, &c. They stay this night, and with them we find an opportunity of going forward as far as Lancaster, which we are determined to embrace.

"Saturday, 27 March, 1790. We stay and get a good breakfast before we set out, and agree to give Mr. Bailey 2s. L. M. for carrying our baggage. This is higher than anything it has cost us on the road in proportion, but we cannot help it. It is better than to waste so much time in a tavern. It rains steadily, and the road is all mush and water. Before I get on a hundred rods I am half-leg deep in mire. Set off about eight o'clock, and overtook the wagon about two miles ahead. However, it clears off before night, and the sun shines warm, and the roads mend fast. We made a stay in Elizabethtown about two hours to feed and rest. The doctor and I had two quarts of beer and some gingerbread and buckwheat cakes for dinner. We got to Colonel Pedens to lodge, which is eighteen miles through an intolerable bad road, to-day. (Elizabethtown, about fifty houses; Middletown, about an hundred houses.) We paid our landlady this evening, as we are to start so early in the morning it would not do to wait till the usual time of getting up to pay then, and we have got nine miles to go to reach Lancaster.

" Lord's Day, 28 March, 1790. We started this morning at day dawn, and got to —— at the Black Horse, four and a half miles to breakfast. The wagon went by us, and fed at Shoop's. I left the doctor with them and to take care of the things, and walked into the town before them. Stopped at Gross's, the Spread Eagle, and left word for the doctor, which they never told him. I heard the bell ring for church just as I got here, which made me go into town after waiting some time for them. Took leave of Mr. Bailey, &c. I went to

the English Episcopal Church, and then
went back to look for the doctor, and he
looking for me; we were some time in
chase, and missed each other. Found we
could not get served at the Angel, so took
our baggage and walked down to Doersh's,
who keeps the stage. Got dinner here.
Shaved, shirted, put on my boots, and went
out into town. Stopped at the court-house
and heard a Methodist. Walked further
about; stopped and looked into the Catholic chapel, and talked with the priest.
Looked into the churches, such as I could,
and returned to tea at sundown. Spent
the remainder of the time till bed reading
newspapers. Washed my feet and went to
bed just before ten.

"Monday, 29 March, 1790. After breakfast the doctor and I took a ramble about
the town, to look at it and to inquire if we
could find any wagon going to Philadelphia, that we can get our baggage carried.
The most likely place we can hear of is to
go to the Creek, about a mile from town.
Immediately after our walk we settled and
paid, and set out at just eleven o'clock.
Paid toll over Conestoga bridge, and

stopped at Locher's, at the Indian King,
two miles from Lancaster, and drank a
quart of beer. It was not good. Dined
at Blesser's, on a cold meal, which was 8*d*.
L. M. apiece. Got to Hamilton's at Sals-
bury, a very good house; nineteen miles.
This is more than I expected when I set
out at eleven o'clock. A very good supper; rye mush and milk, cold corn beef,
and apple pie on the table. But 8*d*. L. M.
for supper and lodging apiece. We have
had very good weather for travelling, and
the roads are drying fast. In hopes that
we shall find some wagon going on the
Philadelphia road, that we may get our
packs carried part of the way.

"Tuesday, 30 March, 1790. We walked
twenty-four miles this day, that is, from
Hamilton's to Fahnstock's. Very pleasant
weather, suitable for travelling; not too
warm nor too cold. My feet very tender
and sore, but we keep along steady. Got
to Fahnstock's, Admiral Warren, about
eight o'clock. Got some bread and milk
for supper. The doctor had nothing but
a pint of cider for his supper. We slept

well, considering my being excessively
fatigued. The post overtook us.

"Wednesday, 31 March.   Stayed to
breakfast this morning, which was very
good, but I do not like the practice, at
least I do not seem to need eating meat
with breakfast every morning. I sometimes eat it two or three times a day because
it is set before me, and it is the fashion to
have meat always on the table. We dined
about seven miles from Philadelphia;
crossed the Schuylkill about sunset, and
walked into town about dark. Crossed the
Schuylkill over the floating bridge, and
paid our toll, 1*d.* Pennsylvania each."

CHAPTER III

A PILGRIM ON BRADDOCK'S ROAD

A YELLOW letter, almost in tatters, lies before me written by one Samuel Allen to his father, Mr. Jason Allen of Montville, New London County, Connecticut, from Bellville, Virginia,[28] November 15, 1796. Bellville is in Wood County, West Virginia, eighteen miles by the Ohio River from Parkersburg.

This letter, describing a journey from Alexandria and Cumberland to the Ohio by way of "broadaggs [Braddock's] old road," gives a picture of certain of the more pathetic phases of the typical emigrant's experience unequaled by any account we have met in print. Incidentally, there is included a mention of the condition of the road and, what is of more interest,

[28] Bellville was the earlier Flinn's Station, Virginia.— S. P. Hildreth's *Pioneer History*, p. 148.

a clear glimpse into the Ohio Valley when the great rush of pioneers had begun after the signing of the Treaty of Greenville, the year before, which ended the Indian War.

"Bellville W. Va November the 15th 1796.
" Honoured Parents

Six months is allmost gone since I left N. London [New London, Connecticut] & not a word have I heard from you or any of the family I have not heard wheather you are dead or alive, sick or well. When I heard that Mr. Backus had got home I was in hopes of recieving a letter by him. but his brother was here the other day and sayes that he left his trunk and left the letters that he had in the trunk, so I am still in hopes of having one yet. There is an opertunity of sending letters once every week only lodge a letter in the post-offis in N. London & in a short time it will be at Belleville. The people that came with me has most all had letters from their friends in New England Mr Avory has had two or three letters from his Brother one in fifteen dayes after date all of whitch came by the waye of the male.

" General Putnam of Muskingdom [Mari-
etta on the Muskingum] takes the New
London papers constantly every week

" When we arrived to Allexandria [Alex-
andria, Virginia] Mr Avory found that
taking land cariag from there to the
Monongehaly would be less expence then
it would be to go any farther up the Potomac & less danger so he hired wagoners
to carry the goods across the mountains to
Morgantown on the Monongahaly about
one hundred miles above Pittsburg Mr
Avorys expence in comeing was from N
London to Allexndria six dollars each for
the passengers and two shillings & six
pence for each hundred weight. from
Allexandria to Morgantown was thirty two
shillings and six pence for each hundred
weight of women & goods the men all
walked the hole of the way. I walked the
hole distance it being allmost three hundred miles and we found the rode to be
pritty good untill we came to the Moun-
taing. crossing the blue Mountain the
Monongehaly & the Lorral Mountains we
found the roads to be verry bad.

" You doubtless remember I rote in my

last letter that Prentice was taken ill a day
or two before   he continued verry much so
untill the 10th of July when he began to
gro wors   the waggoner was hired by the
hundred weight & could not stop unless I
paid him for the time that he stoped & for
the Keeping of the horses that I could not
affoard to do   So we were obliged to keep
on   We were now on the Allegany Mountain & a most horrid rode   the waggon
golted so that I dare not let him ride   So I
took him in my arms and carried him all
the while except once in a while Mr Davis
would take him in his armes & carry him a
spell to rest me.   a young man that Mr
Avory hired at Allexandria a joiner whose
kindness I shall not forgit he kep all the
while with us & spared no panes to assist
us in anything & often he would offer himself.   our child at this time was verry sick
& no medecal assistance could be had on
this mountain   on the morning of the 13th
as we was at breackfast at the house of one
Mr Tumblestone [Tomlinson?] the child
was taken in a fit   our company had gone
to the next house to take breakfast which
was one mile on our way   we were alone

in the room & went & asked Mrs Tumblestone to come into the room   she said she
did not love to see a person in a fitt but
she came into the room   Polly ask her if
she new what was good for a child in a fitt
she said no & immediately left the room &
shut the door after her & came no more
into the room   when that fitt left him there
came on another   no person in the room but
Mr Tumblestone who took but little notis
of the child tho it was in great distress
Polly said she was afraid the child would
die in one of them fitts   Mr Tumblestone
spoke in a verry lite manner and sayes
with a smile it will save you the trouble of
carrying it any farther if it does die   We
then bundled up the child and walked to
the next house ware we come up with our
company   I had just seated myself down
when the child was taken in a fitt again
when that had left it it was immediately
taken in another & as that went off we saw
another coming on   the Man of the house
gave it some drops that stoped the fitt   he
handed me a vial of the dropps — gave
directions how to use them   the child had
no more fitts but seemed to be stuped all

day he cried none at all but he kept a
whining & scouling all the while with his
eyes stared wide open his face and his
eyes appeared not to come in shape as
before When we took dinner it was six
mile to the next house the waggoners said
they could not git through thro that night
we did not love to stay out for fear our
child would die in the woods so we set off
& left the waggons I took the child in my
arms and we traveled on Mr Davis set
off with us & carried the child above half
of the time here we traveled up & down
the most tedious hills as I ever saw & by
nine oclock in the evening we came to the
house the child continued stayed all the
night the next morning at break of day I
heard it make a strange noise I percieved
it grew worse I got up and called up the
women [who] ware with us the woman of
the house got up & in two hours the child
dyed Polly was obliged to go rite off as
soon as his eyes was closed for the waggoners would not stop I stayed to see the
child burried I then went on two of the
men that was with me were joiners & had
their tools with them they stayed with

me & made the coffin   Mr Simkins [Simp-
kins] the man of the house sent his Negroes
out & dug the grave whare he had burried
several strangers that dyed a crossing the
mountain   his family all followed the
corps to the grave black & white & appeared much affected.

" When we returned to the house I asked
Mr Simkins to give me his name & the
name of the place   he asked me the name
of the child   I told him   he took his pen
& ink & rote the following lines Alligany
County Marriland July the 14th 1796 died
John P Allen at the house of John Simkins at atherwayes bear camplain broadaggs old road half way between fort Cumberland & Uniontown.[29]   I thanked him
for the kindness I had received from him

[29] The author has, for several years, been looking for
an explanation of this interesting obituary; " broadaggs " is, clearly, a corruption of " Braddock's." Of
" atherwayes " no information is at hand; it was
probably the name of a woodsman who settled here —
for " bear camplain " undoubtedly means a " bare
campagne," or clearing. The word *campagne* was a
common one among American pioneers. Cf. Harris's
Tour, p. 60.   A spot halfway between Cumberland
and Uniontown would be very near the point where
the road crossed the Pennsylvania state-line.

he said I was verry welcome & he was verry sorry for my loss

"We then proceeded on our journey & we soon overtook the waggons & that nite we got to the foot of the mountain We came to this mountain on the 11th of the month and got over it the 19th at night We left the city of Allexandria on the Potomac the 30th day of June & arrived at Morgantown on the Monongahely the 18th day of July

"Thus my dear pearents you see we are deprived of the child we brought with us & we no not whather the one we left is dead or alive. I beg you to rite & let me no Polly cant bear her name mentioned without shedding tears if she is alive I hope you will spare no panes to give her learning.

"When we arrived at Morgantown the river was so lo that boats could not go down but it began to rain the same day that I got ther I was about one mile from there when it began to rain & from the 22^d at night to the 23^d in the morning it raised 16 feet the logs came down the river so that it was dangerous for boats to go & on Sunday the 22^{d} in the evening the boats set off three waggons had not arrived but the river was loreing so fast that we dare not wate the goods was left with a Merchant in that town to be sent when the river rises they have not come on yet one of my barrels & the brass Cittle is yet behind

" Mr Avory said while he was at Morgantown that Cattle were verry nigh down the river & them that wanted to by he thought had better by then he purchased some & I bought two cows and three calvs for myself & three cows for Mrs Hemsted & calves & a yoke of three year old stears. The next morning after the Boats sailed I set off by land with the cattle & horses with John Turner & Jonathan Prentice & arrived at Bellvill the 9th of August & found it to be a verry rich & pleasant country We came to the Ohio at Wheeling crick one hundred miles belo Pittsburg & about the same from Morgantown We found the country settled the hole of the way from Morgantown to Wheeling & a verry pleasant road we saw some verry large & beautiful plantations

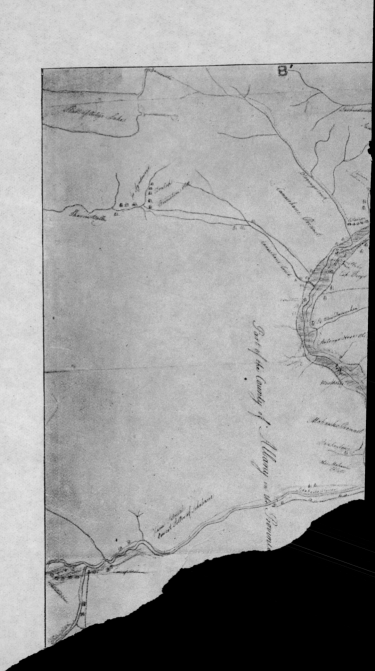

here I saw richer land than I ever saw
before large fields of corn & grane of a
stout groath From Wheeling to Bellville
it is a wilderness for the most of the way
except the banks of the river this side
—— which is one hundred miles we found
it verry difficult to get victules to eat. I
drove fifty miles with one meal of victules
through the wilderness & only a foot path
& that was so blind that we was pestered
to keep it we could drive but a little
wayes in a day whenever night overtook
us we would take our blankets & wrap
around us & ly down on the ground We
found some inhabitance along the river
but they came on last spring & had no
provisions only what they brought with
them

" The country is as good as it was represented to be & is seteling verry fast families are continually moveing from other
parts into this beautiful country if you
would give me all your intrest to go back
there to live again it would be no temta-
tion if you should sell your intrest there
& lay your money out here in a short time I
think you would be worth three or four times

so much as you now are. it is incredible
to tell the number of boats that goes down
this river with familys a man that lives
at Redstone Old fort on the Monongehaly
says that he saw last spring seventy Boats
go past in one day with familys moveing
down the Ohio. There is now at this
place a number of familys that came since
we did from Sesquehanah There is now
at this place eighty inhabitance. Corn is
going at 2.^{s} pr bushel by the quantity 2.^{s}
6-^{d} by the single bushel. There has been
between two & three thousand bushels
raised in Bellville this season & all the
settlements along the river as raised corn
in proportion but the vast number of people that are moveing into this country &
depending upon bying makes it scerce &
much higher than it would be

"There is three double the people that
passes by here then there is by your house
there is Packets that passes from Pittsburg
to Kentucky one from Pittsburg to Wheeling 90 miles one from that to Muskingdom
90 miles One from that to Gallipolees 90
miles the french settlement opisite the big
Canawa [Kanawha] & from that there is

another to Kentucky —— of which goes &
returns every week & —— loaded with
passengers & they carry the male   Mammy
offered me some cloath for a Jacket & if
you would send it by Mr Woodward it
would be very exceptible for cloaths is verry
high here   Common flanel is 6^s per yard &
tow cloth is 3^s 9^d the woolves are so thick
that sheep cannot be kept without a shep-
hard   they often catch   our calvs they
have got one of mine & one of Mrs
Hemstid   the latter they caught in the field
near the houses   I have often ben awoak
out of my sleep by the howling of the
wolves.

"This is a fine place for Eunice   they
ask 1^s per yard for weaving tow cloth   give
my respects to Betsey & Eunice & tell
them that I hope one of them will come
with Mr Woodward when he comes on
Horses are very high in this country & if
you have not sold mine I should be [glad]
if you would try to send him on by Mr.
Woodward.   I dont think Mr Avory will
be there this year or two & anything you
would wish to send you nead not be affraid
to trust to Mr. Woodwards hands for he is

a verry careful & a verry honest man &
what he says you may depend upon.

" Land is rising verry fast   Mr Avory is
selling his lots at 36 dollars apeace   he has
sold three since we came here at that price
we was so long a comeing & provisions so
verry high that I had not any money left
when I got here except what I paid for the
cattle I bought   I have worked for Mr
Avory since I came here to the amount of
sixteen dollars I paid him 80 dollars before
we left N London   I am not in debt to him
at preasent or any one else   I have sot me
up a small house and have lived in it upwards of a fortnight   we can sell all our milk
and butter milk at 2^d per quart   Mr Avory
will give me three shillings per day for
work all winter & find [furnish] me with
victules or 4^s & find myself   I need not
want for business   I think I am worth more
then I was when I came   We have ben in
verry good health ever since we left home.

" General St Clair who is now govener
of the western teritoryes & General Wilkin-
son with their Adicongs [Aid-de-camps]
attended by a band of soldiers in uniform
lodged at Bellvill a few nights ago on their

way from headquarters to Philadelphia
with Amaracan coulours a flying

" Please to give my respects to George
& James & tell them that if they want an
interest this is the country for them to go
to make it   Please to except of my kind
love to yourselves & respects to all friends
who may enquire   do give my love to Mr
Rogers & family & all my brothers and
sisters & our only child Lydia   Polly sends
her love to you & all her old friends &
neighbors

Your affectionate son

Samuel Allen "

The following is a translation of a letter
written twelve years after Washington's
journey of 1784, by Eric Bollman, a
traveler through Dunkard's Bottom, to his
brother Lewis Bollman, father of H. L.
Bollman of Pittsburg:

" From Cumberland we have journeyed
over the Alleghany Mountains in company
with General Irwin, of Baltimore, who
owns some 50,000 acres in this vicinity.
The mountains are not so high and not so
unproductive as I had imagined them to

be.   Several points are rocky and barren, such as the Laurel Ridge, but even this with proper attention and . . European cultivation could be made productive. There are proportionately few such ranges as this, and for the greater part, the mountains are covered with fine timber.

"We spent the first night at West Port. Up to this point, at the proper seasons, the Potomac is navigable and could be made so quite a distance further.   But even in the present state the land journey to the Monongahela, which is navigable and flows into the Ohio, is but a distance of 60 miles.   .   .

"The road is not in a bad condition and could be made most excellent.   This will, without doubt, be accomplished just as soon as the country is sufficiently inhabited, since there is no nearer way to reach the Western waters.

"The next day we dined with Mr. M. McCartin, still higher up in the mountains. There are many settlements in this vicinity. We were entertained in a beautiful, cool, roomy house, surrounded by oat fields and rich meadows, where the sound of the bells told that cattle were pasturing near by. We dined from delicate china, had good knives, good forks, spoons, and other utensils. Our hostess, a bright, handsome, healthy woman, waited upon us. After dinner, a charming feminine guest arrived on horseback; a young girl from the neighboring farm, of perhaps 15 years of age, with such bashful eyes and such rosy cheeks, so lovely and attractive in manner that even Coopley, our good mathematician, could not restrain his admiration.

"This is the 'backwoods' of America, which the Philadelphian is pleased to describe as a rough wilderness — while in many parts of Europe, in Westphalia, in the whole of Hungary and Poland, nowhere, is there a cottage to be found, which, taking all things together in consideration of the inhabitant, can be compared with the one of which I have just written.

"Four miles from this we reached the Glades, one of the most remarkable features of these mountains and this land. These are broad stretches of land of many thousand acres, covered with dense forests;

beyond this there is not a tree to be found, but the ground is covered knee-deep with grass and herbs, where both the botanist and the cattle find delicious food. Many hundred head of cattle are driven yearly, from the South Branch and other surrounding places, and entrusted to the care of the people who live here. What can be the cause of this strange phenomenon! One can only suppose that at one time these glades were covered with timber, which, overthrown by a mighty hurricane, gradually dried and fell into decay. But it would take too long to give the many reasons and arguments both for and against this supposition.

" Only lately have the Indians ceased roving in this vicinity; which has done much to delay its cultivation, but now it is being cleared quite rapidly, and in a short time will, without doubt, become a fine place for pasturage. We spent the second night with one named Boyle, an old Hollander. Early the next morning we could hear the howling of a wolf in the forest.

" We breakfasted with Tim Friend, a hunter, who lived six miles further on.

If ever Adam existed he must have looked as this Tim Friend. I never saw such an illustration of perfect manhood. Large, strong and brawny; every limb in magnificent proportion, energy in every movement and strength in every muscle, his appearance was the expression of manly independence, contentment and intelligence. His conversation satisfied the expectations which it awakened. With gray head, 60 years old, 40 of which he had lived in the mountains, and of an observing mind, he could not find it difficult to agreeably entertain people who wished for information. He is a hunter by profession. We had choice venison for breakfast, and there were around the house and near by a great number of deers, bears, panthers, etc. I cannot abstain from believing that the manly effort which must be put forth in the hunt, the boldness which it requires, the keen observation which it encourages, the dexterity and activity which are necessary to its success, act together more forcibly for the development of the physical and mental strength than any other occupation.

" Agriculture and cattle-raising, in their beginning produce careless customs and indolence; the mental faculties remain weak, the ideas limited, and the imagination, without counterpoise, extravagant. Therefore we admire the wisdom and penetration of the North American Indian, his sublime eloquence and heroic spirit in contrast to the Asiatic shepherd, from whom we receive only simple Arabic fables. The man, of whatever color he may be, is always that which the irresistible influence of his surroundings has formed him. We left our noble hunter and his large, attractive family unwillingly and followed a roadway to Duncard's Bottom, on Cheat river.

" We had ridden along uneventfully for about two hours. I was in advance, when Joseph, who rode behind me, cried: ' Take care, sir. Take care. There is a rattlesnake.' It lay upon the road and my horse had almost stepped upon it, which would have proved a disastrous thing. Joseph, a good active fellow, sprang instantly from his horse in order to kill it. The snake disappeared in the bushes and rattled. It sounded so exactly like the noise of a grasshopper that I did not think it could be anything else. Joseph armed himself with a stout stick and heavy stone, followed the snake, found it, and killed it, but then jumped quickly back, for he saw close by another rattlesnake, which had coiled itself and was ready to spring at him. He hurried back again and killed the second. They were 3½ feet long and nine inches in circumference, in the thickest part of the body; one had nine rattles and the other five. We examined the poisonous fangs, took the rattles with us and hung the bodies on a tree. I had thought until now that the principle of life was as stubborn in a snake as in an eel, but found to my astonishment that a slight blow was sufficient to destroy it in this dangerous specimen. Other observations touching upon natural history I must keep for future discussion.

" We dined at Duncard's Bottom, crossed the Cheat river in the afternoon, reached the Monongahela Valley, spent the night in a very comfortable blockhouse with Mr. Zinn, and arrived the next day at Morgantown, on the Monongahela. We spent a day and a half here and were pleasantly entertained by Mr. Reeder and William M. Clary, and received much information, especially concerning sugar, maple trees and sugar making. From Morgantown we went to the mouth of George creek, Fayette county, Pennsylvania. As it was afternoon when we reached here we were overtaken by night and compelled to spend the night in a small blockhouse with Mr. McFarlain. We found Mr. McFarlain a respectable, intelligent farmer, surrounded as usual, by a large and happy family.

" Directly after our arrival the table was set, around which the entire family assembled. This appears to be the usual custom in the United States with all people who are in some measure in good circumstances. One of the women, usually the prettiest, has the honor of presiding at table. There were good table appointments, fine china, and the simple feast was served with the same ceremony as in the most fashionable society of Philadelphia. Never, I believe, was there in any place more equality than in this. Strangers who come at this time of day at once enter the family circle. This was the case with us. Mr. McFarlain told us much about his farm and the misfortunes with which he struggled when he first cultivated the place upon which he now lives. He has lived here 30 years, a circumstance which is here very unusual, because the adventure loving nature, together with the wish to better their condition and the opportunity, has led many people to wander from place to place.

"'But,' said Mr. McFarlain, when we made this observation, 'I have always believed there was truth in the saying, "A rolling stone gathers no moss." With labor and industry I have at last succeeded, and can still work as well as my sons.'

"'Oh,' said his wife, a jolly woman, 'he does not do much. The most he does is to go around and look at the work.'

"'Let him, let him,' interrupted the daughter, an energetic, pretty girl of perhaps 17 years, who was serving the coffee. 'He worked hard when he was young.' And no girl of finer education could have said it with more charming naivete or with the appearance of more unaffected love.

"After the evening meal the eldest son showed us to our bed-room. 'Shall I close the window?' said he. 'I usually sleep here and always leave it open; it does not harm me, and Dr. Franklin advises it.'

"The next morning when we came down we found the old farmer sitting on the porch reading a paper. Upon the table lay 'Morse's Geography,' 'The Beauty of the Stars,' 'The Vicar of Wakefield,' and other good books. I have entered into particulars in my description of this family, because we were then only five miles from the home of Gallatin, where the people are too often represented as rough, uncultured, good-for-nothings. It is not necessary to mention that all families here are not as this, yet it is something to find a family such as this, living on this side of the mountains, 300 miles from the sea coast. We called upon Mr. Gallatin, but did not find him at home. Geneva is a little place, but lately settled, at the junction of George creek and the Monongahela.

"From here we went to Uniontown, the capital of Fayette county, where we saw excellent land and Redstone creek.

We dined the following day in Redstone or Brownsville; journeyed to Washington, the capital of the county of the same name, and arrived the following day in Pittsburg.

" Of this city and its magnificent situation between two mighty rivers, the Monongahela and the Allegheny, I shall write you another time. From the window where I now sit, I have a view of the first named river, a half mile long. It is as broad as the Thames in London. The bank on this side is high, but horizontal and level, covered with short grass, such as the sheep love, which reminds me of the rock at Brighthelmstein. It is bordered with a row of locust trees. The bank on the other side is a chain of hills, thickly shaded with oak and walnut trees. The river flows quietly and evenly. Boats are going back and forth; even now one is coming, laden with hides from Illinois. The people on board are wearing clothes made of woolen bed blankets. They are laughing and singing after the manner of the French, yet as red as Indians, and almost the antipodes of their fatherland.

" From here to the mouth of the Ohio it

is 1,200 miles and 3,000 to the mouth of the Mississippi. How enormous! How beautiful it is to see the dominion of freedom and common sense established. To see in these grand surroundings the development of good principle and the struggle toward a more perfect life; to admire the spirit of enterprise as it works toward a great plan, which seems to be in relation to the great plan which nature itself has followed, and at last to anticipate by a secret feeling, the future greatness and prosperity which lies before this growing country."

Two years later Felix Renick passed this way and includes in his account a vivid picture of the earliest sort of taverns in the West:

" Some of our neighbors who had served in Dunmore's campaign in 1774, gave accounts of the great beauty and fertility of the western country, and particularly the Scioto valley, which inspired me with a desire to explore it as early as I could make it convenient. I accordingly set out from the south branch of Potomac for that purpose, I think about the first of October, 1798, in company with two friends, Joseph Harness and Leonard Stump, both of whom have long since gone hence. We took with us what provisions we could conveniently carry, and a good rifle to procure more when necessary, and further prepared ourselves to camp wherever night overtook us. Having a long journey before us, we traveled slow, and reached Clarksburgh the third night, which was then near the verge of the western settlements in Virginia, except along the Ohio river. Among our first inquiries of our apparently good, honest, illiterate landlord, was whether he could tell us how far it was to Marietta [Ohio], and what kind of trace we should have? His reply was, ' O yes, I can do that very thing exactly, as I have been recently appointed one of the viewers to lay out and mark a road from here to Marietta, and have just returned from the performance of that duty. The distance on a *straight line* which we first run was seventy-five miles, but on our return we found and marked another line that was much *nearer.*' This theory to Mr. Harness and myself, each of us having spent several years in the study and practice of survey-ing, was entirely new: we however let it pass without comment, and our old host, to his great delight, entertained us till late in the evening, with a detailed account of the fine sport he and his associates had in their bear chases, deer chases, &c., while locating the road. We pursued our journey next morning, taking what our host called the nearest, and which he also said was much the best route. The marks on both routes being fresh and plain, the crooked and nearest route, as our host called it, frequently crossing the other, we took particular notice of the ground the straight line had to pass over, and after getting through we were disposed to believe that our worthy host was not so far wrong as might be supposed. The straight line crossing such high peaks of mountains, some of which were so much in the sugar-loaf form, that it would be quite as near to go round as over them.

" The first night after leaving the settle-ment at Clarksburgh, we camped in the woods; the next morning while our horses were grazing, we drew on our wallets and saddlebags for a snack, that we intended should pass for our breakfast, and set out. We had not traveled far before we unexpectedly came to a new improvement. A man had gone there in the spring, cleared a small field and raised a patch of corn, &c., staying in a camp through the summer to watch it to prevent its being destroyed by the wild animals. He had, a few days before we came along, called on some of his near neighbors on the Ohio, not much more perhaps than thirty miles off, who had kindly came forth and assisted him in putting up a cabin of pretty ample size, into which he had moved bag and baggage. He had also fixed up a rock and trough, and exposed a clapboard to view, with some black marks on it made with a coal, indicating that he was ready and willing to accommodate those who pleased to favor him with a call. Seeing these things, and although we did not in reality need any thing in his way, Mr. Harness insisted on our giving him a call, observing that any man that would settle down in such a wilderness to accommodate travelers ought to

be encouraged. We accordingly rode up
and called for breakfast, horse feed, &c.
Then let me say that as our host had just
 put the ball in motion,' was destitute of
any helpmate whatever, (except a dog or
two,) he had of course to officiate in all the
various departments appertaining to a
hotel, from the landlord down to the shoe-
black on the one side, and from the landlady down to the dishwash on the other.
The first department in which he had to
officiate was that of the hostler, next that
of the bar keeper, as it was then customary,
whether called for or not, to set out a half
pint of something to drink. The next,
which he fell at with much alacrity, was
that of the cook, by commencing with
rolled up sleeves and unwashed hands and
arms, that looked about as black and dirty
as the bears' paws which lay at the cabin
door, part of whose flesh was the most considerable item in our breakfast fare. The
first operation was the mixing up some
pounded corn meal dough in a little black
dirty trough, to which the cleaner, and perhaps as he appeared to think him, the better half of himself, his dog, had free access

before he was fairly done with it, and that
I presume was the only kind of cleaning it
ever got.   While the dodgers were baking,
the bear meat was frying, and what he
called coffee was also making, which was
composed of an article that grew some hundred or one thousand miles north of where
the coffee tree ever did grow.   You now
have the bill of fare that we sat down to,
and the manner in which it was prepared;
but you must guess how much of it we ate,
and how long we were at it.   As soon as
we were done we called for our bill, and
here follows the items: breakfast fifty
cents each, horses twenty-five each, half
pint of whisky fifty cents.   Mr. Harness,
who had prevailed on us to stop, often
heard of the wilderness hotel, and whenever mentioned, he always had some term
of reproach ready to apply to the host and
the dirty breakfast, though we often after-
wards met with fare somewhat similar in
all respects.

" We camped two nights in the woods,
and next day got to Marietta where the
land office was then kept by general Putnam, and from his office we obtained maps

of the different sections of country we
wished to explore."[30]

[30] A reminiscent letter written in 1842 for the *American Pioneer* (vol. i, pp. 73-75).

CHAPTER IV

THE GENESEE ROAD

THE military importance of the Mohawk Valley and strategic portage at Rome, New York, was emphasized in our study of Portage Paths.[31] Throughout the French and Indian War and the Revolutionary struggle the water route to the Hudson from Lake Ontario, by way of the Onondaga, Lake Oneida, Wood Creek, and the Mohawk, was of great moment. But only because it was a route — a thoroughfare; not because the territory through which it coursed was largely occupied or of tremendous value. The French held the lakes and the English were constantly striving for foothold there. When Fort Oswego was built on the present site of Oswego, the first step by the English was taken; the route had been the river route with a portage at Fort Wil-

[31] *Historic Highways of America*, vol. vii, pp. 139-148.

liams (Rome). When Fort Niagara was captured in 1759 by Sir William Johnson, the French were driven from the Lakes; Johnson's route to Niagara was by Lake Ontario from Oswego. It has been suggested that a volume of this series of monographs should be given to the campaigns of the English against Fort Niagara. These campaigns were made largely on waterways; they left no roads which became of any real importance in our national development. Certain campaigns of the Old French War left highways which have become of utmost significance; only of these routes and their story should this series be expected to treat. Despite the two wars which had created busy scenes in the Mohawk Valley, no landward route connected it with Niagara River and Lake Erie except the Iroquois Trail.[32] No military road was built through the "Long House of the Iroquois." To gain the key of the western situation — Niagara — the common route was to Oswego. There were local roads along the lake shore, and these were used

[32] *Historic Highways of America*, vol. ii, pp. 76–85.

more or less by the troops.   In the Revolution no American general could get beyond Fort Stanwix by land.   Leger himself came up the Oswego River to join Burgoyne.

As a consequence, the interior of New York was an almost unexplored wilderness at the end of the Revolution in 1783. With the opening of the Genesee country by the various companies which operated there, a tide of immigration began to surge westward from the upper Mohawk along the general alignment of the old-time Iroquois Trail.   Utica sprang up on the site of old Fort Schuyler, and marked the point of divergence of the new land route of civilization from the water route.[33]   This was about 1786.   In 1789 Asa Danworth erected his salt works at Bogardus Corners, now the city of Syracuse.   Geneva, Batavia, and Buffalo mark the general line of the great overland route from Utica and Syracuse across New York.   It followed very closely the forty-third meridian, dropping somewhat to reach Buffalo.

The Great Genesee Road, as it was early

[33] The Iroquois Trail likewise left the river valley at this spot.

known, began at old Fort Schuyler, as a
western extremity of the Mohawk Valley
road and later turnpike, and was built to
the Genesee River by a law passed March
22, 1794. In 1798 a law was passed extending it to the western boundary of the
state. It was legally known as the Great
Genesee Road and the Main Genesee Road
until 1800. In that year the road passed
into the hands of a turnpike company the
legal name of which was " The President
and Directors of the Seneca Road Company." The old name clung to the road
however, and on the map here reproduced
we find it called the " Ontario and Genesee
Turnpike Road." It forms the main street
of both the large cities through which it
passes, Syracuse and Utica, and in both it
is called " Genesee Street."

The first act of legislation which created
a Genesee Road from an Indian trail read
as follows:

"*Be it enacted by the People of the State of
New York, represented in Senate and Assembly*
That Israel Chapin, Michael Myer, and
Othniel Taylor shall be and hereby are
appointed commissioners for the purpose

of laying out and improving a public road
or highway to begin at Old Fort Schuyler
on the Mohawk river and to run from
thence in a line as nearly straight as the
situation of the country will admit to the
Cayuga Ferry in the county of Onondaga
or to the outlet of the Cayuga lake at the
discretion of the said commissioners and
from the said outlet of the Cayuga lake or
from the said Cayuga Ferry as the same
may be determined on by the said commissioners in a line as nearly straight as
the situation of the country will admit to
the town of Canadaquai and from thence
in a line as nearly straight as possible to
the settlement of Canawagas on the Genesee river.

"*And be it further enacted* That the said
road shall be laid out six rods wide, but it
shall not be necessary for the said commissioners to open and improve the same
above four rods wide in any place thereof.
And the whole of the said road when laid
out, shall be considered as a public highway and shall not be altered by the commissioners of any town or country [county?]
through which the same shall run.

"*And be it further enacted* That the treasurer of this State shall pay to the said commissioners or any two of them a sum or sums of money not exceeding in the whole the sum of six hundred pounds out of the monies in the treasury which have arisen or may arise from the sale of military lotts to be laid out and expended towards the opening and improving that part of the said road passing through the military lands.

"*And be it further enacted* That for the purpose of laying out opening and improving the remainder of the said road, the said treasurer shall pay unto the said commissioners or any two of them out of any monies in the treasury not otherwise appropriated at the end of the present session of the legislature a sum not exceeding fifteen hundred pounds which said sum shall be by them laid out and expended in making or improving the remainder of the said road as aforesaid. *Provided* that no larger proportion of the said sum of fifteen hundred pounds shall be appropriated towards the opening and improving of the said road in the county of Ontario then in the county of Herkemer.

"*And be it further enacted* That it shall
and may be lawful to and for the said commissioners or any two of them to improve
the said road by contract or otherwise as to
them may appear the most proper.

"*And be it further enacted* That where
any part of the said road shall be laid out
through any inclosed or improved lands
the owner or owners thereof shall be paid
the value of the said lands so laid out into
an highway with such damages as he, she
or they may sustain by reason thereof
which value and damages shall be settled
and agreed upon by the said commissioners
or any two of them and the parties interested therein, and if they cannot agree,
then the value of the lands and damages
shall be appraised by two justices of the
peace, on the oaths of twelve freeholders
not interested in paying or receiving any
part of such appraisement, otherwise than
in paying their proportion of the taxes for
the contingent charges of the county which
freeholders shall be summoned by any
constable not otherwise interested than as
aforesaid, by virtue of a warrant to be is-
sued by the said two justices of the peace

for that purpose, and the whole value of the said lands so laid out into an highway, and damages together with the costs of ascertaining the value of the said damages of the county in which the said lands shall be situated are levied collected and paid.

"*And be it further enacted* That each of the said commissioners shall be entitled to receive for their services the sum of sixteen shillings for every day they shall be respectively employed in the said business to be paid by the respective counties in which they shall so be employed which sums shall be raised levied and paid together with and in the same manner as the necessary and contingent charges of such county are raised levied and paid and that the said commissioners shall account with the auditor of this State for the monies they shall respectively receive from the treasurer of this State by virtue of this act on or before the first day of January one thousand seven hundred and ninety six." [34]

A law entitled "An act appropriating monies for roads in the county of Onondaga

[34]*Laws of New York*, 1794, ch. XXIX.

and for other purposes therein mentioned,''
passed April 11, 1796, contained the following concerning the Genesee Road:

"*And be it further enacted* That the said
commissioners shall and they are hereby
strictly enjoined to expend two thousand
dollars of the said monies in repairing the
highway and bridges thereon heretofore
directed to be laid out by law and now
commonly called the Great Genesee road
from the eastern to the western bounds of
the said county of Onondaga and the resi-
due of the money aforesaid to expend in the
repair of such highways and the bridges
thereon in the said county as will tend
most extensively to benefit and accommodate the inhabitants thereof.

"*And be it further enacted* That it shall be
the duty of the said commissioners and
they are hereby strictly enjoined to cause
all and every bridge which shall be constructed under their direction over any
stream to be raised at least three feet
above the water at its usual greatest height
in the wettest season of the year and to
construct every such bridge of the most
durable and largest timber which can be

obtained in its vicinity, and that wherever it can conveniently be done the road shall be raised in the middle so as to enable the water falling thereon freely to discharge therefrom and shall pursue every other measure which in their opinion will best benefit the public in the expenditure of the money committed to them." [35]

In an act, passed April 1, 1796, supplementary to an " Act for the better support of Oneida, Onondaga and Cuyuga Indians . . ", it was ordered that from the proceeds of all sales of lands bought of the Indians the surveyor-general should pay £500 to the treasurer of Herkimer County and a like amount to the treasurer of Onondaga County; this money was ordered to be applied to " mending the highway commonly called the Great Genesee Road and the bridges thereon." [36]

A law of the year following, 1797, affords one of the interesting uses of the lottery in the development of American highways. It reads:

" Whereas it is highly necessary, that

[35] *Laws of New York*, 1796, ch. XXVI.
[36] *Id.*, ch. XXXIX.

direct communications be opened and improved between the western, northern and southern parts of this State.   Therefore

"Be it enacted by the People of the State of New York, represented in Senate and Assembly, That for the purpose of opening and improving the said communications, the managers herein after named shall cause to be raised by three successive lotteries of equal value, the sum of forty-five thousand dollars.   That out of the neat [net?] proceeds of the first lottery the sum of eleven thousand seven hundred dollars, and out of the neat proceeds of the third lottery, the further sum of two thousand two hundred dollars shall be and hereby is appropriated for opening and improving the road commonly called the Great Genesee road, in all its extent from Old Fort Schuyler in the county of Herkimer to Geneva in the county of Ontario.   .   . " [37]

The western movement to Lake Erie became pronounced at this time; the founders of Connecticut's Western Reserve under General Moses Cleaveland emigrated in 1796.   The promoters of the Genesee

[37]*Laws of New York*, 1797, ch. LX.

country were advertising their holdings widely. The general feeling that there was a further West which was fertile, if not better than even the Mohawk and Hudson Valleys, is suggested in a law passed March 2, 1798, which contained a clause concerning the extension of the Genesee Road:

"*And be it further enacted* That the commissioner appointed in pursuance of the act aforesaid, to open and improve the main Genessee road, shall and he is hereby authorized and empowered to lay out and continue the main Genessee road, from the Genessee river westward to the extremity of the State. *Provided nevertheless*, that none of the monies appropriated by the said act shall be laid out on the part of the road so to be continued; *and provided also* that the said road shall be made at the expense of those who may make donations therefor." [38]

The mania which swept over the United States between 1790 and 1840 of investing money in turnpike and canal companies was felt early in New York. The success of the

[38] *Laws of New York*, 1798, ch. XXVI.

Lancaster Turnpike in Pennsylvania was the means of foisting hundreds of turnpike-road companies on public attention and private pocket-books. By 1811, New York State had at least one hundred and thirty-seven chartered roads, with a total mileage of four thousand five hundred miles, and capitalized at seven and a half millions.

It is nothing less than remarkable that this thoroughfare from the Mohawk to Lake Erie should have been incorporated as a turnpike earlier in point of time than any of the routes leading to it (by way either of the Mohawk Valley or Cherry Valley) from Albany and the East. The Seneca Road Company was incorporated April 1, 1800. The Mohawk Turnpike and Bridge Company was incorporated three days later. The Cherry Valley routes came in much later.

The Genesee Road was incorporated by the following act, April 1, 1800:

" An act to establish a turnpike road company for improving the State road from the house of John House in the village of Utica, in the county of Oneida, to the village of Cayuga in the county of Cayuga, and from thence to Canadarque in the county of Ontario.

"*Be it enacted by the People of the State of New York represented in Senate and Assembly* That Benjamin Walker, Charles Williamson, Jedediah Sanger and Israel Chapin and all such persons as shall associate for the purpose of making a good and sufficient road in the form and manner herein after described from the house of John House .   . observing as nearly the line of the present State [Genesee] road as the nature of the ground will allow, shall be and are hereby made a corporation and body politic in fact and in name, by the name of ' The President and Directors of the Seneca Road Company'.   .   ."[39]

The road was to be under the management of nine directors and the capital stock was to be two thousand two hundred shares worth fifty dollars each. The directors were empowered to enter upon any lands necessary in building the road, specifications being made for appraisal of damages. The road was to "be six rods in width .   . cleared of all timber except-

[39] *Laws of New York*, 1797–1800, ch. LXXVIII.

ing trees of ornament, and to be improved
in the manner following, to wit, in the
middle of the said road there shall be
formed a space not less than twenty four
feet in breadth, the center of which shall
be raised fifteen inches above the sides,
rising towards the middle by gradual arch,
twenty feet of which shall be covered with
gravel or broken stone fifteen inches deep
in the center and nine inches deep on the
sides so as to form a firm and even surface.''

Tollgates were to be established when
the road was in proper condition every ten
miles; the rates of toll designated in this
law will be of interest for comparative
purposes:

Tolls in 1800 on Seneca Turnpike, New York

Wagon, and two horses	.12½
Each horse additional	.03
Cart, one horse	.06
Coach, or four wheeled carriage, two horses	.25
Each horse additional	.03
Carriage, one horse	.12½
Each horse additional	.06
Cart, two oxen	.08
Each yoke additional	.03
Saddle or led horse	.04
Sled, between December 15 and March 15	.12½
Score of cattle	.06
Score of sheep or hogs	.03

The old Genesee Road passed through as romantic and beautiful a land as heart could wish to see or know; but the road itself was a creation of comparatively modern days, in which Seneca and Mohawk were eliminated factors in the problem. Here, near this road, a great experiment was made a few years after its building, when a canal was proposed and dug, amid fears and doubts on the part of many, from Albany to Buffalo. One of the first persons to advocate a water highway which would eclipse the land route, sent a number of articles on the subject to a local paper, whose editor was compelled to refuse to print more of them, because of the ridicule to which they exposed the paper! Poor as the old road was in bad weather, people could not conceive of any better substitute.

When the Erie Canal was being built, so poor were the roads leading into the region traversed by the canal, that contractors were compelled to do most of their hauling in winter, when the ground was frozen and sleds could be used on the snow. Among the reasons given — as we shall see in a later monograph of this series — for delays

in completing portions of the canal, was that of bad roads and the impossibility of sending heavy freight into the interior except in winter; and a lack of snow, during at least one winter, seriously handicapped the contractors. But when the Erie Canal was built, the prophecies of its advocates were fulfilled, as the rate per hundredweight by canal was only one-tenth the rate charged by teamsters on the Genesee Road. The old "waggoners" who, for a generation, had successfully competed with the Inland Lock Navigation Company, could not compete with the Erie Canal, and it was indeed very significant that, when Governor Clinton and party made that first triumphal journey by canal-boat from Buffalo to Albany and New York — carrying a keg of Lake Erie water to be emptied into the Atlantic Ocean — they were not joyously received at certain points, such as Schenectady, where the old methods of transportation were the principal means of livelihood for a large body of citizens. How delighted were the old tavern-keepers in central New York with the opening of the Erie Canal, on whose boats immigrants

ate and slept? About as happy, we may
say, as were the canal operators when a
railway was built, hurrying travelers on at
such a rapid pace that their destinations
could be reached, in many cases, between
meals!

Yet until the railway came, the fast mail-
stages rolled along over the Genesee Road,
keeping alive the old traditions and the old
breed of horses. Local business was vastly
increased by the dawning of the new era;
society adapted itself to new and altered
conditions, and the old days when the
Genesee Road was a highway of national
import became the heritage of those who
could look backward and take hope for the
future, because they recognized better the
advances that each new year had made.

CHAPTER V

A TRAVELER ON THE GENESEE ROAD

AMONG the many records of travelers on the famous Genesee Road, that of Timothy Bigelow, as given in his *Journal of a Tour to Niagara Falls in the Year 1805*,[40] approaches perhaps most nearly to the character of a description of the old highway which should be presented here:

"July 14th. We proceeded [from Albany] to Schenectady to breakfast, fifteen miles, Beale's tavern; a good house. A new turnpike is making from Albany to this place; it is constructed in a very durable manner, with a pavement covered with hard gravel. That part which is completed is now an excellent road; the remainder will soon be equally good. It was not disagreeable to us to be informed that this road, and indeed all the other turnpikes, and most other recent works which we met

---

[40] Boston, 1876, pp. 11–53.

with, which required uncommon ingenuity or labor, were constructed by Yankees.

"Schenectady seems not to be a word fitted to common organs of speech. We heard it pronounced Snacketady, Snackedy, Ksnackidy, Ksnactady, Snackendy, and Snackady, which last is much the most common. To Ballston, Bromeling's, sixteen miles; a most excellent house. We found here about forty guests, but understood there were upwards of two hundred at Aldrich's, McMasters's, and the other boarding-houses near. Bromeling himself has accommodations in the first style for one hundred and thirty persons.

"We met with but few people here from Massachusetts. Mr. Henry Higginson and his wife, Mr. Bingham, the bookseller, and his family, were all we knew. The mineral water was not agreeable to us all upon the first experiment; but with others, and myself in particular, it was otherwise. It is remarkably clear and transparent; the fixed air, which is continually escaping from it, gives it a sparkling appearance, and a lively and full taste, not unlike to that of brisk porter or champagne wine,

while one is actually drinking. . .
We slept at Beals's. July 17th, we took
the western stage in company with a Mr.
Row, a gentleman from Virginia, who was
about to engage in trade at Geneva, on the
Seneca Lake. We crossed over to the
north side of the Mohawk soon after
setting out, to Schwartz's (still in Schenectady), a poor house, seven miles; thence
to Pride's in Amsterdam, nine miles.
Pride's is a handsome limestone house,
built about fifty years since, as we were
informed, by Sir William Johnson, for his
son-in-law, Guy Johnson. . . To
Abel's in Amsterdam, situated on Trapp's
Hill, opposite to the mouth of Schoharie
River and the old Fort Hunter, to dine.
The prospect to the south-west is extensive
and romantic, exhibits an agreeable mixture of hills and plains, diversified with
extensive forests almost in a state of nature, and cultivated fields scarce less extensive, now covered with a rich harvest of
ripening wheat. The prospect was the
principal thing which we found in this
place to recommend it. The tavern is a
poor one, and our dinner of course was

miserable. Four miles to Shepard's, in
Canajoharie, to sleep.   .   . The Mohawk in many places was shoal, and interrupted with so many islands and sand-
banks that we were often at a loss to conceive how loaded boats could pass, and yet
we saw several going up-stream with
heavy loads.   .   . July 18th. To
Carr's at Little Falls, to breakfast, twenty
miles; a very good house. In this stage,
we passed the East Canada Creek. Observed for the very first time the cypress-
tree. The gloomy, melancholy air of this
tree, and the deep shade which it casts,
resulting from the downward direction of
its branches, as well as the form and color
of its leaves, have very properly marked it
out as emblematical of mourning.

" On approaching the Little Falls, we
observed undoubted marks of the operation
of the water on rocks, now far out of their
reach, particularly the round holes worn
out [by] pebbles kept in a rotatory motion
by the current, so common at all falls. It
is certain that heretofore the falls must
have been some ways further down stream,
and have been much greater than they

now are, and that the German flats, and
other low grounds near the river above,
must have been the bed of a lake. The
falls occupy about half a mile. In some
spots, the river is so crowded between
rocks, that one might almost pass across it;
in most places, however, it is broken into
a number of streams by irregular masses
of limestone rock. There is here a commodious canal for the passage of boats cut
round these falls. The whole fall is fifty-
four feet; and there are five locks, in each
of which the fall is ten feet, besides the
guard-lock, where it is four. The locks
are constructed of hewn stone, and are of
excellent workmanship; they are almost
exactly upon the construction of those at
the head of Middlesex canal. Most of the
buildings in the neighborhood, as well as
two beautiful bridges over the canal here,
are also of limestone. Carr and his wife
are from Albany, and are agreeable and
genteel people.

" To Trowbridge's Hotel, in Utica, to
dine. The house is of brick, large, commodious, and well attended. We found
good fare here; in particular, excellent

wine. From Little Falls to this is twenty-two miles. In this stage, we passed the German flats, an extensive and well-cultivated tract of internal land on both sides the Mohawk. The town of German Flats is on the south of the town of Herkimer, opposite thereto, on the north side of the river. Notwithstanding the celebrity of this spot for the excellence of its soil, we thought it not equal to that on Connecticut River. Having passed the West Canada Creek, the hills on both sides the river seem to subside, and open to the view an extensive and almost unbounded tract of level and fertile country, though of a much newer aspect than any we had seen before.

" At Utica, we passed over to the southern side of the Mohawk. The river here is about the size of the Nashua, and from this place bends off to the north-west. We happened to pass the bridge as a batteau was coming up to a store at the end of it, to discharge its cargo. The water was so shoal that the batteau grounded before it could be brought to its proper place. A pair of horses were attached to its bows, and it was not without the assistance of

several men, added to the strength of the horses, that it was got up to the landing-place at last.

" Morality and religion do not seem to have much hold of the minds of people in this region. Instances of rudeness and profanity are to be met with in almost every place, but the people engaged in unloading the batteau were much more extravagantly and unnecessarily profane than is common. Several persons also, whom I saw at Little Falls this morning, told me that they knew full well that Adam could not have been the first man, or that he must have lived much longer ago than the Scriptures declare, because they said it must be more than five thousand years for the Mohawk to have broken through the rocks, as it has done at those falls.

" Utica was begun to be settled sixteen years ago, and is now a little city, and contains several elegant dwelling-houses, some of which are of brick, and a few of stone, together with a great number of stores and manufactories of different kinds. The Lombardy poplar-tree is cultivated here in great abundance. The facility of transportation by means of the Mohawk and Hudson Rivers on one side, and Wood Creek, Oneida, and Ontario Lakes on the other, together with the extraordinary fertility of the adjacent country, must at no great distance of time make Utica a place of great business and resort, and of course its population must rapidly increase. Moses Johnson, a broken trader, late of Keene, now of Manlius, a little above this place, whom we saw at Trowbridge's, spoke of this country as not favorable for traders, and that a very few stores of goods would overstock the market. It is natural, however, for people in his situation to ascribe their misfortunes to anything rather than their own imprudence or misconduct, which others would probably consider as the true cause of them. Mr. Charles Taylor and his father, whom we had overtaken at Shepard's, we left at Utica.

" July 19th. To Laird's in Westmoreland, to breakfast, eleven miles; a very good house. Our breakfast here was garnished with a dish of excellent honey.

Every thing in and about the house was neat, and we were particularly struck with the genteel and comely appearance of two young ladies, daughters of our landlord, one of whom, we were told, had attended a ball in the neighborhood, I think at Paris, the evening before. This stage was over a tract of very fertile country, nearly level, but a little ascending; the growth was mostly of rock-maple and lime-tree. We passed a creek in New Hartford, called Sawguet, or Sogwet, or Sacada [Sauquoit], and another in a corner of Paris called Kerry, or Riscana, say Oriskany. The whole country from Utica to this place is thickly settled. The houses are mostly well built, and many of them handsome; very few log houses to be seen. Young orchards are numerous and thrifty, and Lombardy poplars line the road a great part of the way; and yet we saw not a single field which had not the stumps of the original forest trees yet remaining in it. Honey is sent from hence to Lake Ontario, in barrels.

" To Shethar's in Sullivan, eighteen miles, to dine; a good tavern. The face

of the country is not so level here as about
Utica, though it cannot be called hilly,
even here. In addition to the forest trees
which we had before seen, we here found
the shag-bark nut tree in abundance. In
this stage, we passed through the Oneida
Indian village. . . In this stage,
we also passed the Skanandoa Creek, the
first water we met with which discharges
itself into the ocean by the St. Lawrence,
as the Oriskany was the last which pays
tribute to the Hudson.

" We next passed the Oneida Creek,
which unites with the Skanandoa. The
earth in some places here is of the same
color with that on Connecticut River,
where the red freestone is found. In the
Oneida village, the fields are free from
stumps, the first to be met that are so from
Utica to this place. . . To Tyler's
in Onondaga Hollow, to sleep, twenty-one
miles. The last sixteen miles are over a
very hilly country; the Canaseraga Mountain, in particular, is four or five miles
over, and very steep. . .

" The country, as we approached Onondaga Hollow, we found had been longer

settled than nearer the Oneida village,
because the last cession of the Oneidas on
the west, and immediately contiguous to
their present reservation, was made but six
or eight years ago, whereas the country to
the westward of that had begun to be settled
some time before.   The town of Manlius,
in particular, has the appearance of a flourishing settlement.   This town is the first
in the *Military Tract*, which is the lands
given by the State of New York as a gra-
tuity to the officers and soldiers of their
line in the Revolutionary Army.   As we
were descending into the Onondaga Hollow, we saw to the north-westward the
Salina or Onondaga Lake.   .   .

" The Onondaga Creek, which is of a
convenient size for a mill-stream, runs
along the Hollow from south to north, as
do all the other streams in this country.
This creek passes near the celebrated Onondaga salt springs, which are situated about
five   or   six   miles   northward   from
Tyler's.   .   . July 20th. Rose at
half past two o'clock, and proceeded to
Andrew's, at Skaneateles, to breakfast, sixteen miles; a good tavern.   The country

is still hilly, but very fertile. The soil is deep,— a mixture of loam and clay. The roads here must be very bad in wet weather. It rained last night for the first time since we commenced our journey; and the horses' feet, in consequence thereof, slipped as if they were travelling on snow or ice.

" Rising out of Onondaga Hollow is a long and very steep hill. The road is constructed on the southern side of a precipice, in such a manner that, as you approach the top of the hill, you have a tremendous gulf on your left hand, at the bottom of which you hear the murmur of a brook fretting among the rocks, as it is passing on toward the Onondaga Creek, which it joins in the Hollow. There is a kind of railing or fence, composed of logs secured with stakes or trees, which is all that prevents the passenger, and even the road itself, from falling to the bottom of the gulf. On the hill we found the embryo of a village. A court-house is already built, and the frame of a hotel is raised. The hotel, we were told, is to be kept by one Brunson. It is an

accommodation much needed by travellers
on this road.

" To Harris's in Cayuga, fifteen miles,
to dine. We here had an excellent dinner
of beefsteaks. Mr. Harris told us that
they could keep beef fresh four or five
days, in hot weather, by hanging it upon
the trees — wrapping it in flannel — as
high as was convenient. Flannel is better
to wrap it in than linen.

" The village of Cayuga is small, but
pleasant and lively. It is in the township
of Marcellus, on the eastern bank of the
Cayuga Lake, within one or two miles of
its northern extremity. This lake is about
two miles wide in general, and almost forty
miles long. Nearly north and south from
the village, there are about fifteen miles of
the lake in sight. The shores are mostly of
hard land, except at the northern extremity, where there is a great deal of marsh,
which is an unfavorable circumstance for
the village, as it is not only disagreeable to
the sight, but, I think, also to the smell.
There is a wooden bridge across the lake,
leading from Cayuga village towards
Geneva, one mile long, wanting three

roods. It suffered so much by shocks of
the ice last winter, that in some places it
is hardly safe to pass it. This forenoon we
had passed the outlet of the Owasco Lake,
but did not see the lake itself, which we
were told was about a mile south of the
road. The country hitherto is somewhat
uneven, though by no means so much so
as near the Onondaga Hollow. The soil,
however, is excellent in many places, and
is of a reddish color.

" To Powell's Hotel in Geneva, to sleep,
sixteen miles; excellent accommodations.
At Harris's we had met with a Mr. Rees,
a gentleman in trade at Geneva, who took
passage in the stage with us for that place.
From this gentleman, whom we found very
intelligent and communicative, we learned
many particulars concerning the salt
springs, discovered about five years since
upon the Cayuga outlet. These springs
are about twelve miles below the Cayuga bridge, and are on both sides
the outlet: that on the western side is in
the township of Galen, and belongs to Mr.
Rees and his partner in trade. These
springs had long been known to the

Indians, but they had always been reserved
in communicating their knowledge of the
state of the country to the white settlers.
It was not till most or all of those who
lived near this outlet had died or moved
away, except one, that he mentioned the
existence of these springs; and for a re-
ward he conducted some persons to the
place where they are situated. The persons to whom he communicated this information endeavored to purchase the favored
spot before the owner should be apprised
of its inestimable value; but he accidentally
obtained a knowledge of his good fortune,
and of course refused to sell.   .   .

The road from Cayuga to Geneva is for a
few miles along the southern or south-
eastern side, and the rest along the northern or north-eastern side of the Seneca
outlet. The face of the country near the
road is more level; but the soil is more
sandy and uninviting than we had lately
seen, till we approached near to Geneva.
The land there is excellent, as we were
told it was, through all the tract which
extends between the Cayuga and Seneca
Lakes. This tract rises in a kind of regu-

lar glacis from each lake, so that from the middle of it one can see both. It wants nothing but inhabitants and cultivation to make it an elysium. The Seneca outlet flows into the lower end of the Cayuga Lake. Towards its mouth there is a considerable fall, or rather rapid, which it is contemplated to lock, whereby a water communication will be opened between the two lakes. The stream is about half the size of the Winnipiseogee, and has a bluish-white appearance.

" We were within half a mile of Geneva before we came in sight of the Seneca Lake. This charming sheet of water extends southerly from this place to Catharine Town, forty miles, being from two to four miles wide. There is not a foot of swamp or marsh on its borders, from one extremity to the other; but it is everywhere lined by a clear, gravelly beach, and the land rises from it with a very gentle and graceful ascent in every direction. . .

" Not far from Geneva are some of the Indian orchards, which were cut down by General Sullivan in his famous expedition, scarce less barbarous than those of the

savages themselves.   The trees now growing in these orchards sprouted from the
roots of those which were cut down, and
therefore grow in clusters, six or seven
rising from one root.   We saw Indian
fields here free from stumps, the only ones
which are to the westward of Utica, except
those belonging to the Oneidas.   We were
told that, at this season of the year, the
wind at Geneva blows constantly from the
south in the forenoon, and from the north
in the afternoon.   We here quitted the
stage, which runs no further than Canandaigua, and hired an open Dutch wagon
and driver, and a single horse, to carry us
to Niagara.   .   .   The turnpike road
ends at this place [Canandaigua].   The
whole length from Albany is two hundred
and six or seven miles: it may properly be
called two turnpikes, which join each other
at Utica.   A project is on foot for still
extending the turnpike even to Niagara, a
direct course to which would not probably
exceed one hundred miles.

" Mr. Rees told us yesterday that he
was engaged to proceed to-morrow with
certain commissioners to mark out the

course of the road, and that the proprietors
will begin to work upon it next year.
The road may not be very good property
at first, but will probably soon become so,
judging from the astonishing rapidity with
which this country is settled. It is ascer-
tained that one thousand families migrated
hither during the last year, two thirds of
whom were from New England.

" To Hall's in Bloomfield, to sleep,
twelve miles; very good house. We had
an excellent supper and clean beds. The
town of Bloomfield has been settled about
fifteen years, and is now in a flourishing
state. Here is a handsome new meeting-
house with a tasty steeple. The vane on
the steeple is rather whimsical. It is a
flying angel, blowing a trumpet against the
wind. . . To Hosmer's in Hart-
ford, to breakfast, twelve and a half miles.
Between Bloomfield and this, we passed
through Charleston, which has but recently
been reclaimed from the wilderness. It is
perfectly flat, the soil is pretty good, though
better, and more settled at some distance
from the road than near it. The reason
of cutting the road where it goes was be-

cause the country in that direction was
open, when it was first explored, between
this place and Lake Ontario, which is but
twenty-eight miles distant, or to Gerun-
degut [now Toronto] Bay, but twenty-two
miles.   .   .

" Hitherto we have found better roads
since we left the turnpike than before, except that the bridges and causeways are
mostly constructed with poles. Hosmer,
our landlord, is an intelligent man and
keeps a good tavern. We had for breakfast good coffee, excellent tea, loaf sugar,
mutton chop, waffles, berry pie, preserved
berries, excellent bread, butter, and a salad
of young onions. I mention the particulars, because some of the articles, or such
a collection, were hardly to be expected in
such a depth of wilderness.

" To Gansen's in Southampton, twelve
and a half miles, to dine. Within about a
mile of Hosmer's, we passed the Genesee
River. The outlet of the Conesus Lake
joins this river about a mile above, or to
the south. Where we crossed, there is a
new bridge, apparently strong and well
built; and yet the water last spring under-

mined one end of it, so that it has sunk
considerably.   .   .

"Gansen's is a miserable log house. We
made out to obtain an ordinary dinner.
Our landlord was drunk, the house was
crowded with a dozen workmen, reeking
with rain and sweat, and we were, withal,
constantly annoyed with the plaintive and
frightful cries and screams of a crazy
woman, in the next room. We hastened
our departure, therefore, even before the
rain had ceased.

"To Russell's in Batavia, twelve miles,
to sleep. One mile from Gansen's, we
crossed Allen's Creek, at Buttermilk Falls,
where there are mills, and five miles
further the Chookawoonga Creek, near the
eastern transit line of the Holland purchase. This line extends from the bounds
of Pennsylvania to Lake Ontario, a distance
of near ninety-four miles. So far, the road
was the worst of any we had seen; and
none can be much worse and be passable
for wheels. Within six miles of Batavia,
the road is much better, and the land of
a good quality, heavily timbered all the
way, but especially near the settlement. It

is but three years since this spot was first
cleared, and it is now a considerable village. Here is a large building, nearly
finished, intended for a court-house, jail,
and hotel, under the same roof. The
street is perfectly level, and is already a
good and smooth road. Here is also an
excellent mill, on a large and commodious
scale, situated on the Tonawanda Creek,
which is the first water we saw which
passes over Niagara Falls. Russell's is a
poor tavern. We were told that our sheets
were clean, for they had been slept in but
a *few* times since they were washed.

" July 23d. To Luke's in Batavia, to
breakfast, five miles. We intended to have
stopped at McCracken's, one mile short of
this, but we were told that we could not be
accommodated. The exterior appearance
of both houses was very much alike; they
are log huts, about twelve feet square.
Luke's consisted of a single room, with a
small lean-to behind, which served for a
kitchen. It contained scarce any furniture,
not even utensils enough to serve us comfortably for breakfast.   .   .   .

" It was but eighteen months since Luke

began a settlement here, and he was the first who made the attempt between Batavia and Vandevener's, a distance of eighteen miles, though in that distance now there are several huts. Taverns like Luke's are not uncommon in this vicinity; almost every hut we saw had a sign hung out on a pole or stump, announcing that it was an inn. Perhaps such complete poverty did not exist in them all as we found at Luke's, yet, judging from external appearances, the difference could not be great.

" We passed the Tonawanda near Batavia court-house, and then kept along its southern bank to this place. The woods are full of new settlers. Axes were resounding, and the trees literally falling about us as we passed. In one instance, we were obliged to pass in a field through the smoke and flame of the trees which had lately been felled and were just fired.

" To Vandevener's in Willink, thirteen miles. We had intended only to dine here; but by reason of a thunder shower, and the temptation of comfortable accommodations, we concluded not to proceed till next day. Our last stage was through the

Batavia woods, famed for their horrors, which were not abated by our having been informed at Russell's, that not far from here a white man had lately been killed by the Indians. We found the road much better than we had anticipated; the last four miles were the worst. A little labor would make the road all very good, at least in dry weather. There is another way to come from Batavia here; but it is six miles further, and probably little or no better than this.

" It was but three years since Vandevener began here. He at first built a log house, but he has now a two-story framed house, adjoining that. His whole territory is five hundred acres, one hundred of which he has already got under improvement.   .   .

" July 23d. To Ransom's in Erie, to breakfast, fourteen miles. Ransom came from Great Barrington in Massachusetts, and settled here last September.   .   .
The last three miles from Ellicott's Creek to Ransom's is a new road cut through a thick wood, and is as bad as any part of the road through the Batavia woods.

" To Crow's at Buffalo Creek, eight

miles. In this stage, we passed the Four Mile Creek. Half the distance from Ransom's was over open country, . . in which many young chestnut-trees are just sprouting from the ground. The rest of our way was through a thick wood, where the growth is the same kind as in the interior of Massachusetts. . .

" From Buffalo we passed along the beach of Lake Erie, to the ferry across its outlet on the Niagara River, at Black Rock, so called, three miles. . ."

CHAPTER VI

THE CATSKILL TURNPIKE

SO few writers have paid any attention to the influence of roads in the development of our country that it is a great pleasure to find in Francis Whiting Halsey's *The Old New York Frontier*,[41] a chapter on the old Catskill Turnpike; through the kindness of the author it is possible to present here this story of that strategic highway of old New York:

" Before the Revolutionary War something of a road had been cut through the woods from Otsego Lake southward along the Susquehanna, and other primitive roads led to and from the lake; but these highways had almost disappeared during the later years of the war, when Nature had done her effective work of reclamation. The one leading from the lake southward was improved in 1786 as far as Hartwick, and others were speedily taken in hand.

[41] Published by Charles Scribner's Sons, 1901.

Further down the river efforts were made
to establish convenient communication
with the Hudson, and out of this grew a
road which eventually became the great
highway for a large territory. It was called
the Catskill Turnpike, and had its terminus
on the Susquehanna at Wattles's Ferry.[41*]

" This road, as a turnpike, properly
dates from 1802, but the road itself is much
older. Its eastern end had been opened
long before the Revolution with a terminus
in the Charlotte Valley. It seems then to
have been hardly more than a narrow
clearing through the forest, what farmers
call a ' wood road,' or frontiersman a
' tote road.' It served as a convenient
route to the Susquehanna, because much
shorter than the older route by the Mohawk
Valley. Over this road on horseback in
1769, came Colonel Staats Long Morris and
his wife, the Duchess of Gordon.

" After the war demands rose for a better road, and one was soon undertaken

[41.] This name long since was abandoned. On the
opposite side of the river, however, a new settlement
grew up under the name of Unadilla, the beginnings of
which date about 1790. See the same author's "The
Pioneers of Unadilla Village " (Unadilla, 1902).–HALSEY.

with its terminus at Wattles's Ferry.
This terminus appears to have been chosen
because the river here was deep enough to
permit the use of ' battoes ' during the
low water that prevailed in summer. By
the summer of 1788 the road was in passable condition. Alexander Harper and Ed-
ward Paine in February, 1789, declared
that they had been to ' a very great expense in opening the roads from Catskill
and the Hudson to the Susquehanna
River.' In the same year a petition was
filed for a road ' from the Ouleout to
Kyuga Lake.' The road to Cayuga Lake
(Ithaca) made slow progress, and in 1791
General Jacob Morris addressed to Governor Clinton a letter which shows that it
was then still to be undertaken. Early in
1790 the State had taken the road to
Catskill in charge. In August, G. Gelston
made up from surveys a map from Catskill
' running westerly to the junction of the
Ouleout Creek with the Susquehanna
River.' The country had been previously
explored for the purpose by James Barker
and David Laurence.[42]

[42] State Land Papers. — HALSEY.

"In 1791 Sluman Wattles charged his cousin, Nathaniel Wattles, £4, 6s. for 'carting three barrells from your house to Catskill,' £1 for 'five days work on the road,' and 15 shillings for 'inspecting road.' Besides Nathaniel Wattles, Menad Hunt was interested in the work, and in 1792 the two men appealed to the state to be reimbursed for money paid out above the contract price.[43] During this year the father of the late Dr. Samuel H. Case, of Oneonta, emigrated to the upper Ouleout from Colchester, Conn., with his seven brothers. They drove cattle and sheep ahead of them, and consumed eight days in making the journey from the Hudson River. Solomon Martin went over the road in the same year, using Sluman Wattles's oxen, for which he was charged £1, 17s. He went to Catskill, and was gone fifteen days. This road was only twenty-five feet wide. In 1792 a regular weekly mail-route was established over it.

"These are among the many roads which were opened in the neighborhood before the century closed — before the Catskill

[43] Sluman Wattles's Account Book. — HALSEY.

Turnpike, as a turnpike, came into existence. Nearly every part of the town of
Unadilla, then embracing one-third of
Otsego County, had been made accessible
before the year 1800. The pioneers had
taken up lands all through the hill country.
But the needs of the settlers had not been
fully met. All over the State prevailed
similar conditions. The demands that
poured in upon State and town authorities
for road improvements became far in excess
of what could be satisfied. Everywhere
fertile lands had been cleared and sown to
grain, but the crops were so enormous that
they could neither be consumed at home
nor transported to market elsewhere.
Professor McMaster says that ' the heaviest
taxes that could have been laid would not
have sufficed to cut out half the roads or
build half the bridges that commerce
required.

" Out of this condition grew the policy
of granting charters to turnpike companies,
formed by well-to-do land-owners, who
undertook to build roads and maintain
them in proper condition for the privilege
of imposing tolls. Men owning land and

possessed of ready money, were everywhere eager to invest in these enterprises.
They not only saw the promise of divi-
dends, but ready sales for their lands. At
one time an amount of capital almost equal
to the domestic debt of the nation when
the Revolution closed was thus employed
throughout the country. By the year
1811, no fewer than 137 roads had been
chartered in New York State alone, with a
total length of 4,500 miles and a total capital of $7,500,000. About one-third of this
mileage was eventually completed.

"Eight turnpikes went out from Albany,
and five others joined Catskill, Kingston,
and Newburg with the Susquehanna and
Delaware rivers. The earliest of these
five, and one of the earliest in the State,
was the Catskill and Susquehanna turnpike, that supplanted the primitive State
road to Wattles's Ferry. The old course
was changed in several localities, the charter permitting the stockholders to choose
their route. Among the names in the
charter were John Livingston, Caleb Benton (a brother of Stephen Benton), John
Kortright, Sluman Wattles, and Solomon

Martin.   The stock was limited to $12,000 in shares of $20 each.

" The road ran through lands owned by the stockholders.   Little regard was had for grades, as travellers well know.   The main purpose was to make the land accessible and marketable.   The road was completed in 1802, and soon became a famous highway to Central New York, and the navigable Susquehanna, and so remained for more than a quarter of a century.   It was in operation four years earlier than the Great Western Turnpike, connecting Albany with Buffalo and running through Cherry Valley.   Spafford in 1813 described it as ' the Appian Way turnpike,' in which it seems the pride felt in it, likened as it thus was to one of the best roads ever built by man — that Roman highway which still does service after the lapse of more than 2,000 years.   In one sense this turnpike was like a Roman road: it followed straight lines from point to point regardless of hills, obstacles being squarely faced and defied by these modern mèn as by the old Romans.

" Ten toll-gates were set up along the

line, with the rates as follows: for twenty
sheep and hogs, eight cents; for twenty
horses and cattle, twenty cents; for a
horse and rider, five cents; for a horse
and chaise, twelve and one-half cents; for
a coach or chariot, twenty-five cents; for
a stage or wagon, twelve and one-half
cents. In 1804, Caleb Benton, who lived
in Catskill, was president of the corporation, and in 1805 the stage business of the
road was granted as a monopoly to David
Bostwick, Stephen Benton, Lemuel Hotch-
kiss, and Terence Donnelly. Two stages
were to be kept regularly on the road, the
fare to be five cents per mile. A stage that
left Catskill Wednesday morning reached
Unadilla Friday night, and one that left
Unadilla Sunday reached Catskill Tuesday.
The most prosperous period for the road
was the ten years from 1820 to 1830.

" Two years after the road was built, Dr.
Timothy Dwight, President of Yale Col-
lege, during one of his regular vacation
journeys, passed over it and stopped at
Unadilla. He has left a full record of the
journey. Dr. Dwight, accustomed long to
the comforts of life in New England, had

no sooner crossed the State line from
Massachusetts to New York than he observed a change. The houses became
ordinary and ill repaired, and very many
of them were taverns of wretched appearance.

" For sixteen or eighteen miles, he saw
neither church nor school-house. Catskill
contained about 100 houses, and much of
the business was done by barter. The
turnpike to the Susquehanna he described
as a ' branch of the Greenwood turnpike
from Hartford to Albany, commencing
from Canaan in Connecticut and passing to
Wattles's Ferry on the Susquehanna.
Thence it is proposed to extend it to the
county of Trumbull on the southern shore
of Lake Erie.' The road he thought ' well
made.'

" Connecticut families were found settled
along the line. Now he came upon ' a few
lonely plantations recently begun upon the
road,' and then ' occasionally passed a cottage, and heard the distant sound of an axe
and of a human voice. All else was
grandeur, gloom and solitude.' At last
after many miles of riding he reached a

settlement ' for some miles a thinly built
village, composed of neat, tidy houses,' in
which everything ' indicated prosperity.'
This was Franklin. Coming down the
Ouleout, the country, he said, ' wore a
forbidding aspect, the houses being thinly
scattered and many of them denoted great
poverty.'

"When Dr. Dwight reached Wattles's
Ferry, the more serious trials of his journey
began. All the privations of life in a new
country which he had met on the road
from Catskill at last had overtaxed his
patience, and he poured forth his per-
turbed spirit upon this infant settlement.
When he made a second visit a few years
later he liked the place much better. His
first impressions are chronicled at some
length. He says:

" ' When we arrived at the Susquehanna
we found the only inn-keeper, at the eastern side of the river, unable to furnish us
a dinner. To obtain this indispensable
article we were obliged therefore to cross
the river. The ferry-boat was gone. The
inhabitants had been some time employed
in building a bridge, but it was un-

finished and impassable. There was nothing left us, therefore, but to cross a deep and rapid ford. Happily the bottom was free from rocks and stones.'

" Dr. Dwight appears to have found no satisfactory stopping-place in Unadilla, and proceeds to say:

" ' About four miles from the ferry we came to an inn kept by a Scotchman named Hanna. Within this distance we called at several others, none of which could furnish us a dinner. I call them inns because this name is given them by the laws of the State, and because each of them hangs out a sign challenging this title. But the law has nicknamed them, and the signs are liars.

" ' It is said, and I suppose truly, that in this State any man who will pay for an inn-keeper's license obtains one of course. In consequence of this practice the number of houses which bear the appellation is enormous. Too many of them are mere dramshops of no other use than to deceive, disappoint and vex travellers and to spread little circles of drunkenness throughout the State. A traveller after passing from

inn to inn in a tedious succession finds that
he can get nothing for his horse and nothing for himself.'

" The remedy he prescribed for this was
to license ' only one inn where there are
five or six.' The evil was general. In
1810 the people of Meredith made a formal
and vigorous protest against the growth of
intemperance and crime as caused by public houses. There were ten hotels in that
town alone, besides a number of distilleries.
Many citizens banded themselves in behalf
of order and decency, and their protest
abounded in an energy of language that
would have delighted the soul of Dr.
Dwight. Of his further experience at Mr.
Hanna's hotel, he says:

" ' We at length procured a dinner and
finding no house at a proper distance
where we could be lodged concluded to
stay where we were. Our fare was indeed
bad enough, but we were sheltered from
the weather. Our inn-keeper besides
furnishing us with such other accommodations as his home afforded, added to it the
pleasures of his company and plainly considered himself as doing us no small favor.

In that peculiar situation in which the tongue vibrates with its utmost ease and celerity, he repeated to us a series of anecdotes dull and vulgar in the extreme. Yet they all contained a seasoning which was exquisite, for himself was in every case the hero of the tale. To add to our amusement, he called for the poems of Allan Ramsay and read several of them to us in what he declared to be the true Scottish pronunciation, laughing incessantly and with great self-complacency as he proceeded.'

" Dr. Dwight remarks that ' a new turnpike road is begun from the ferry and intended to join the Great Western road either at Cayuga bridge or Canandaigua. This route will furnish a nearer journey to Niagara than that which is used at present.' We see from this what were the plans of that day, as to the future central highway of New York State. Of Unadilla Dr. Dwight says:

" ' That township in which we now were is named Unadilla and lies in the county of Otsego. It is composed of rough hills and valleys with a handsome collection of inter-

vales along the Susquehanna. On a remarkably ragged eminence immediately
north-west of the river, we saw the first
oaks and chestnuts after leaving the neighborhood of Catskill. The intervening
forests were beach, maple, etc. The
houses in Unadilla were scattered along the
road which runs parallel with the river.
The settlement is new and appears like
most others of a similar date. Rafts con-
taining each from twenty to twenty-five
thousand feet of boards are from this township floated down the Susquehanna to
Baltimore. Unadilla contained in 1800
eight hundred and twenty-three inhabitants.'[44]

"On September 27, 1804, Dr. Dwight
left Mr. Hanna's inn and rode through to
Oxford. The first two miles of the way
along the Susquehanna were 'tolerably
good and with a little labor capable of
being excellent.' He continues:

"'We then crossed the Unadilla, a river
somewhat smaller but considerable longer

[44]Dr. Dwight's figures are for the township, not for
the village, which was then a mere frontier hamlet, of
perhaps one hundred souls. — HALSEY.

(sic) than the Susquehanna proper, quite as
deep and as difficult to be forded. Our
course to the river was south-west. We
then turned directly north along the banks
of the Unadilla, and travelling over a
rugged hill, passed through a noble cluster
of white pines, some of which though not
more than three feet in diameter, were, as
I judged, not less than 200 feet in height.
No object in the vegetable world can be
compared with this.'

" Eleven years later, Dr. Dwight again
passed over the turnpike on his way to
Utica. ' The road from Catskill to Oxford,' he said, ' I find generally bad, as
having been long neglected. The first
twenty miles were tolerable, the last twenty
absolutely intolerable.' After noting that
in Franklin ' religion had extensively prevailed,' he wrote:

" ' Unadilla is becoming a very pretty
village. It is built on a delightful ground
along the Susquehanna and the number of
houses, particularly of good ones, has much
increased. A part of the country between
this and Oxford is cultivated; a considerable part of it is still a wilderness. The

country is rough and of a high elevation.'

"In some reminiscences[45] which my father wrote in 1890, he described the scenes along this road that were familiar to him in boyhood at Kortright — 1825 to 1835. The road was then in its most prosperous period. It was not uncommon for one of the hotels, which marked every few miles of the route, to entertain thirty or forty guests at a time. The freight wagons were huge in size, drawn by six and eight horses, and had wheels with wide tires. Stages drawn by four and six horses were continually in use. Not infrequently came families bound for Ohio, where they expected to settle — some of these Connecticut people, who helped to plant the Western Reserve settlements. This vast traffic brought easy prosperity to the people along the turnpike and built up towns and villages. My father records the success of the Rev. Mr. McAuley's church at Kortright — a place that has now retrograded so that it is only a small hamlet, just capa-

[45] " Reminiscences of Village Life and of Panama and California from 1840 to 1850," by Gains Leonard Halsey, M. D. Published at Unadilla. — HALSEY.

ble of retaining a post office. But Mr.
McAuley's church at one time, more than
sixty years ago, had five hundred mem-
bers, and was said to be the largest church
society west of the Hudson valley.

" A change occurred with the digging of
the Erie Canal and the building of the Erie
Railway. Morever, in 1834 was built a
turnpike from North Kortright through the
Charlotte Valley to Oneonta. The white
man having tried a route of his own over
the hills, reverted to the route which the
red man had marked out for him ages
before. Much easier was the grade by this
river road, and this fact exercised a marked
influence on the fortunes of the settlements
along the olden line. Freight wagons
were drawn off and sent by the easier way.
Stages followed the new turnpike and the
country between Wattles's Ferry and Kortright retrograded as rapidly as it had
formerly improved.[46]

" The building of the Catskill Turnpike
really led to the founding of Unadilla vil-

[46] A stage line, however, for long years afterward sup-
plied these settlements with a means of communication
with Unadilla, and it is within the memory of many

lage on its present site. It had confined to
this point a growth which otherwise would
probably have been distributed among
other points along the valley. Here was a
stopping-place, with a river to be crossed,
horses to be changed, and new stages
taken, and here had been established the
important market for country produce of
Noble & Hayes. Unadilla became what
might be called a small but thriving inland
river port. Here lumber was sawed and
here it came from mills elsewhere for ship-
ment along with farm products to Baltimore. Here grain was ground, and here
were three prosperous distilleries.

"The building of the turnpike along the
Charlotte was not the only blow that came
to the western portion of the Catskill Road.
Another and permanent one came to the
whole length of the turnpike when the Erie

persons still calling themselves young that for a considerable series of years, trips twice a week were regularly made by Henry S. Woodruff. After Mr. Woodruff's death a large and interesting collection of coaches,
sleighs, and other stage relics remained upon his
premises — the last survival of coaching times on the
Catskill Turnpike, embracing a period of three-quarters
of a century. — HALSEY.

Canal was built, followed later by the Erie Railroad. Otsego County, in 1832, had reached a population of 52,370, but with the Erie Canal in operation it ceased to grow. At the present time the showing is considerably less than it was in 1832, and yet several villages have made large increases, the increase in Oneonta being probably tenfold.

"Contemporary with the Erie Canal was an attempt to provide the Susquehanna with a canal. It became a subject of vast local interest from Cooperstown to the interior of Pennsylvania. The scheme included a railway, or some other method of reaching the Erie Canal from the head of Otsego Lake. Colonel De Witt Clinton, Jr., son of the governor, made a survey as far as Milford, and found that in nine miles there was a fall of thirty feet, and that at Unadilla the fall from the lake was 150 feet, while in 110 miles from the lake it was 350 feet. In 1830 a new survey showed that 144 miles out of 153 were already navigable, the remaining distance requiring a canal. Some seventy locks would be needed and sixty-five dams.

Judge Page, while a member of Congress, introduced a bill to aid slack-water navigation from Cooperstown to tide-water. It was his opinion that the failure of the bill was due to the spread of railroads.

" With the ushering in of the great railroad era, the Susquehanna Valley saw started as early as 1830 many railroad projects which could save it from threatened danger. Their aim was to connect the upper Susquehanna with the Hudson at Catskill, and the Mohawk at Canajoharie. None ever got beyond the charter stage. Strenuous efforts were afterward made to bring the Erie from the ancient Cookoze (Deposit) to the Susquehanna at a point above Oghwaga, but this also failed.

" Indeed it was not until after the Civil War that any railroad reached the headwaters of the Susquehanna; but it was an agreeable sign of the enterprise which attended the men of 1830 and following years that at the period when the earliest railroad in this State, and one of the earliest on this continent, had just been built from Albany to Schenectady, serious projects existed for opening this valley to the outer world. Even the great Erie project languished long in consequence of business depression. It was not until 1845 that it was completed as far as Middletown, and not until 1851 that it reached Dunkirk.

"Not even to the Erie was final supremacy on this frontier assured, but the upper Susquehanna lands, more than those through which the Erie ran, were doomed to a condition of isolation. Nature itself had decreed that the great route of transportation in New York State was to run where the great trail of the Iroquois for centuries had run — through the Mohawk Valley. Along that central trail from Albany, ' the Eastern Door,' to Buffalo, ' the Western door of the Long House,' the course of empire westward was to take its way."

CHAPTER VII

WITH DICKENS ALONG PIONEER ROADS

SOME of the most interesting descriptions of pioneer traveling are from the racy pages of Charles Dickens's *American Notes*, a volume well known to every reader. No description of early traveling in America would be complete, however, without including a number of these extremely witty, and, in some instances, extremely pathetic descriptions of conditions that obtained in Virginia and Ohio in Dickens's day. The following description of a negro driver's manipulation of reins, horses, and passengers may be slightly exaggerated, but undoubtedly presents a typical picture of southern stage driving:

"Soon after nine o'clock we come to Potomac Creek, where we are to land; and then comes the oddest part of the journey. Seven stage-coaches are preparing to carry us on.   Some of them are ready, some of them are not ready.   Some of the drivers are blacks, some whites.   There are four horses to each coach, and all the horses, harnessed or unharnessed, are there. The passengers are getting out of the steamboat, and into the coaches, the luggage is being transferred in noisy wheelbarrows; the horses are frightened, and impatient to start; the black drivers are chattering to them like so many monkeys; and the white ones whooping like so many drovers: for the main thing to be done in all kinds of hostlering here, is to make as much noise as possible.   The coaches are something like the French coaches, but not nearly so good.   In lieu of springs, they are hung on bands of the strongest leather. There is very little choice or difference between them; and they may be likened to the car portion of the swings at an English fair, roofed, put upon axle-trees and wheels, and curtained with painted canvas. They are covered with mud from the roof to the wheel-tire, and have never been cleaned since they were first built.

" The tickets we have received on board

the steamboat are marked No. 1, so we
belong to coach No. 1. I throw my coat
on the box, and hoist my wife and her maid
into the inside. It has only one step, and
that being about a yard from the ground, is
usually approached by a chair: when there
is no chair, ladies trust in Providence.
The coach holds nine inside, having a seat
across from door to door, where we in England put our legs: so that there is only one
feat more difficult in the performance than
getting in, and that is getting out again.
There is only one outside passenger, and
he sits upon the box. As I am that one, I
climb up; and while they are strapping
the luggage on the roof, and heaping it
into a kind of tray behind, have a good
opportunity of looking at the driver.

" He is a negro — very black indeed.
He is dressed in a coarse pepper-and-salt
suit excessively patched and darned (particularly at the knees), grey stockings, enormous unblacked high-low shoes, and very
short trousers. He has two odd gloves:
one of parti-coloured worsted, and one of
leather. He has a very short whip, broken
in the middle and bandaged up with

string. And yet he wears a low-crowned, broad-brimmed, block hat: faintly shadowing forth a kind of insane imitation of an English coachman! But somebody in authority cries ' Go ahead!' as I am making these observations. The mail takes the lead in a four-horse wagon, and all the coaches follow in procession: headed by No. 1.

" By the way, whenever an Englishman would cry ' All right!' an American cries ' Go ahead!' which is somewhat expressive of the national character of the two countries.

" The first half mile of the road is over bridges made of loose planks laid across two parallel poles, which tilt up as the wheels roll over them: and IN the river. The river has a clayey bottom and is full of holes, so that half a horse is constantly disappearing unexpectedly, and can't be found again for some time.

" But we get past even this, and come to the road itself, which is a series of alternate swamps and gravel-pits. A tremendous place is close before us, the black driver rolls his eyes, screws his mouth up very round, and looks straight between the two leaders, as if he were saying to himself, ' We have done this often before, but *now* I think we shall have a crash.' He takes a rein in each hand; jerks and pulls at both; and dances on the splashing board with both feet (keeping his seat, of course) like the late lamented Ducrow on two of his fiery coursers. We come to the spot, sink down in the mire nearly to the coach windows, tilt on one side at an angle of forty-five degrees, and stick there. The insides scream dismally; the coach stops; the horses flounder; all the other six coaches stop; and their four-and-twenty horses flounder likewise: but merely for company, and in sympathy with ours. Then the following circumstances occur.

" BLACK DRIVER (to the horses). ' Hi! '

Nothing happens. Insides scream again.

BLACK DRIVER (to the horses). ' Ho! '

Horses plunge, and splash the black driver.

GENTLEMAN INSIDE (looking out). ' Why, what on airth —'

Gentleman receives a variety of splashes and draws his head in again, without finishing his question or waiting for an answer.

BLACK DRIVER (still to the horses).
'Jiddy! Jiddy!'

Horses pull violently, drag the coach out
of the hole, and draw it up a bank; so
steep, that the black driver's legs fly up
into the air, and he goes back among the
luggage on the roof.   But he immediately
recovers himself, and cries (still to the
horses),

'Pill!'

No effect.   On the contrary, the coach
begins to roll back upon No. 2, which rolls
back upon No. 3, which rolls back upon No.
4, and so on, until No. 7 is heard to curse
and swear, nearly a quarter of a mile behind.

BLACK DRIVER (louder than before).
'Pill!'

Horses make another struggle to get up
the bank, and again the coach rolls backward.

BLACK DRIVER (louder than before).
'Pe-e-e-ill!'

Horses make a desperate struggle.

BLACK DRIVER (recovering spirits).   'Hi!
Jiddy, Jiddy, Pill!'

Horses make another effort.

BLACK DRIVER (with great vigour).
'Ally Loo! Hi. Jiddy, Jiddy. Pill. Ally
Loo!'

Horses almost do it.

BLACK DRIVER (with his eyes starting
out of his head). 'Lee, dere. Lee, dere.
Hi. Jiddy, Jiddy. Pill. Ally Loo.
Lee-e-e-e-e!'

"They run up the bank, and go down
again on the other side at a fearful pace.
It is impossible to stop them, and at the
bottom there is a deep hollow, full of water.
The coach rolls frightfully. The insides
scream. The mud and water fly about us.
The black driver dances like a madman.
Suddenly we are all right by some extraordinary means, and stop to breathe.

"A black friend of the black driver is
sitting on a fence. The black driver recog-
nizes him by twirling his head round and
round like a harlequin, rolling his eyes,
shrugging his shoulders, and grinning
from ear to ear. He stops short, turns to
me, and says:

"'We shall get you through sa, like a
fiddle, and hope a please you when we get
you through sa. Old 'ooman at home sir:'

chuckling very much. ' Outside gentleman sa, he often remember old 'ooman at
home sa,' grinning again.

" ' Aye aye, we'll take care of the old
woman. Don't be afraid.'

" The black driver grins again, but there
is another hole, and beyond that, another
bank, close before us. So he stops short:
cries (to the horses again) ' Easy. Easy
den. Ease. Steady. Hi. Jiddy. Pill.
Ally. Loo!' but never ' Lee!' until we
are reduced to the very last extremity, and
are in the midst of difficulties, extrication
from which appears to be all but impossible.

" And so we do the ten miles or there-
abouts in two hours and a half; breaking
no bones though bruising a great many;
and in short getting through the distance,
' like a fiddle.'

" This singular kind of coaching termi-
nates at Fredericksburgh, whence there is
a railway to Richmond.   .   ."

Dickens, the student of human nature,
surely found vast material for inspection
and observation in our American coaches.
The drivers particularly attracted his attention as we have seen; their philosophical

indifference to those under their charge as
well as their anxieties on certain occasions
caused him to marvel. The stage-drivers
of Dickens's day were marvels and offer
character studies as unique as they were
interesting. For the general air of con-
scienceless indifference on the part of
drivers, and exasperated verbosity of
passengers, perhaps no sketch of Dickens is
more to the point than the following which
describes, with lasting flavor, a ride from
York, Pennsylvania, to Harrisburg:

" We left Baltimore by another railway
at half-past eight in the morning, and
reached the town of York, some sixty miles
off, by the early dinner-time of the Hotel
which was the starting-place of the four-
horse coach, wherein we were to proceed
to Harrisburg.

" This conveyance, the box of which I
was fortunate enough to secure, had come
down to meet us at the railroad station, and
was as muddy and cumbersome as usual.
As more passengers were waiting for us at
the inn-door, the coachman observed under
his breath, in the usual self-communica-
tive voice, looking the while at his mouldy

harness, as if it were to that he was addressing himself:

"' I expect we shall want *the big* coach.'

"I could not help wondering within myself what the size of this big coach might be, and how many persons it might be designed to hold; for the vehicle which was too small for our purpose was something larger than two English heavy night coaches, and might have been the twin-brother of a French diligence. My speculations were speedily set at rest, however, for as soon as we had dined, there came rumbling up the street, shaking its sides like a corpulent giant, a kind of barge on wheels. After much blundering and backing, it stopped at the door: rolling heavily from side to side when its other motion had ceased, as if it had taken cold in its damp stable, and between that, and the having been required in its dropsical old age to move at any faster pace than a walk, were distressed by shortness of wind.

"' If here ain't the Harrisburg mail at last, and dreadful bright and smart to look at too,' cried an elderly gentleman in some excitement, ' darn my mother!'

" I don't know what the sensation of being darned may be, or whether a man's mother has a keener relish or disrelish of the process than anybody else; but if the endurance of this mysterious ceremony by the old lady in question had depended on the accuracy of her son's vision in respect to the abstract brightness and smartness of the Harrisburg mail, she would certainly have undergone its infliction. However, they booked twelve people inside; and the luggage (including such trifles as a large rocking-chair, and a good-sized dining-table), being at length made fast upon the roof, we started off in great state.

" At the door of another hotel, there was another passenger to be taken up.

" ' Any room, sir?' cries the new passenger to the coachman.

" ' Well there's room enough,' replies the coachman, without getting down, or even looking at him.

" ' There an't no room at all, sir,' bawls a gentleman inside. Which another gentleman (also inside) confirms, by predicting that the attempt to introduce any more passengers ' won't fit nohow.'

" The new passenger, without any expression of anxiety, looks into the coach, and then looks up at the coachman: ' Now, how do you mean to fix it?' says he, after a pause: ' for I *must* go.'

" The coachman employs himself in twisting the lash of his whip into a knot, and takes no more notice of the question: clearly signifying that it is anybody's business but his, and that the passengers would do well to fix it, among themselves. In this state of things, matters seem to be approximating to a fix of another kind, when another inside passenger in a corner, who is nearly suffocated, cries faintly,

" ' I'll get out.'

" This is no matter of relief or self-congratulation to the driver, for his immoveable philosophy is perfectly undisturbed by anything that happens in the coach. Of all things in the world, the coach would seem to be the very last upon his mind. The exchange is made, however, and then the passenger who has given up his seat makes a third upon the box, seating himself in what he calls the middle: that is, with half his person on my legs, and the other half on the driver's.

"'Go a-head cap'en,' cries the colonel, who directs.

"'Go-lang!' cries the cap'en to his company, the horses, and away we go.

"We took up at a rural bar-room, after we had gone a few miles, an intoxicated gentleman who climbed upon the roof among the luggage, and subsequently slipping off without hurting himself, was seen in the distant perspective reeling back to the grog-shop where we had found him. We also parted with more of our freight at different times, so that when we came to change horses, I was again alone outside.

"The coachmen always change with the horses, and are usually as dirty as the coach. The first was dressed like a very shabby English baker; the second like a Russian peasant; for he wore a loose purple camlet robe with a fur collar, tied round his waist with a parti-coloured worsted sash; grey trousers; light blue gloves; and a cap of bearskin. It had by this time come on to rain very heavily, and

there was a cold damp mist besides, which
penetrated to the skin. I was very glad to
take advantage of a stoppage and get down
to stretch my legs, shake the water off my
great-coat, and swallow the usual anti-
temperance recipe for keeping out the
cold.   .   .

" We crossed this river [Susquehanna]
by a wooden bridge, roofed and covered in
on all sides, and nearly a mile in length.
It was profoundly dark; perplexed, with
great beams, crossing and recrossing it at
every possible angle; and through the
broad chinks and crevices in the floor, the
rapid river gleamed, far down below, like
a legion of eyes. We had no lamps; and
as the horses stumbled and floundered
through this place, towards the distant
speck of dying light, it seemed intermin-
able. I really could not at first persuade
myself as we rumbled heavily on, filling
the bridge with hollow noises, and I held
down my head to save it from the rafters
above, but that I was in a painful dream;
for I have often dreamed of toiling through
such places, and as often argued, even at
the time, ' this cannot be reality.'

" At length, however, we emerged upon
the streets of Harrisburg.   .   ."

Coachmen are further described by Dickens during his stagecoach trip from Cincin-
nati to Columbus in Ohio:

" We often stop to water at a roadside
inn, which is always dull and silent.   The
coachman dismounts and fills his bucket,
and holds it to the horses' heads.   There
is scarcely any one to help him; there are
seldom any loungers standing round; and
never any stable-company with jokes to
crack.   Sometimes, when we have changed
our team, there is a difficulty in starting
again, arising out of the prevalent mode of
breaking a young horse; which is to catch
him, harness him against his will, and put
him in a stage-coach without further notice:
but we get on somehow or other, after a
great many kicks and a violent struggle;
and jog on as before again.

" Occasionally, when we stop to change,
some two or three half-drunken loafers
will come loitering out with their hands in
their pockets, or will be seen kicking their
heels in rocking-chairs, or lounging on the
window sill, or sitting on a rail within the

colonnade: they have not often anything to say though, either to us or to each other, but sit there idly staring at the coach and horses. The landlord of the inn is usually among them, and seems, of all the party, to be the least connected with the business of the house. Indeed he is with reference to the tavern, what the driver is in relation to the coach and passengers: whatever happens in his sphere of action, he is quite indifferent, and perfectly easy in his mind.

"The frequent change of coachmen works no change or variety in the coachman's character. He is always dirty, sullen, and taciturn. If he be capable of smartness of any kind, moral or physical, he has a faculty of concealing it which is truly marvellous. He never speaks to you as you sit beside him on the box, and if you speak to him, he answers (if at all) in monosyllables. He points out nothing on the road, and seldom looks at anything: being, to all appearance, thoroughly weary of it, and of existence generally. As to doing the honours of his coach, his business, as I have said, is with the horses. The coach follows because it is attached to them and goes on wheels: not because you are in it. Sometimes, towards the end of a long stage, he suddenly breaks out into a discordant fragment of an election song, but his face never sings along with him: it is only his voice, and not often that.

"He always chews and always spits, and never encumbers himself with a pocket-handkerchief. The consequences to the box passenger, especially when the wind blows toward him, are not agreeable."

Hiring a special express coach at Columbus, Dickens and his party went on to Sandusky on Lake Erie alone. His description of the rough, narrow corduroy road is unequaled and no one but Dickens could have penned such a thrilling picture of the half-conquered woodland and its spectral inhabitants:

" There being no stage-coach next day, upon the road we wished to take, I hired ' an extra,' at a reasonable charge, to carry us to Tiffin, a small town from whence there is a railroad to Sandusky. This extra was an ordinary four-horse stage-coach, such as I have described, changing horses and drivers, as the stage-coach would, but

was exclusively our own for the journey.
To ensure our having horses at the proper
stations, and being incommoded by no
strangers, the proprietors sent an agent on
the box, who was to accompany us all the
way through; and thus attended, and bearing with us, besides, a hamper full of
savoury cold meats, and fruit, and wine;
we started off again, in high spirits, at
half-past six o'clock next morning, very
much delighted to be by ourselves, and
disposed to enjoy even the roughest
journey.

" It was well for us, that we were in this
humour, for the road we went over that
day, was certainly enough to have shaken
tempers that were not resolutely at Set
Fair, down to some inches below Stormy.
At one time we were all flung together in
a heap at the bottom of the coach, and at
another we were crushing our heads
against the roof. Now, one side was down
deep in the mire, and we were holding on
to the other. Now, the coach was lying on
the tails of the two wheelers; and now it
was rearing up in the air, in a frantic state,
with all four horses standing on the top of

an insurmountable eminence, looking coolly
back at it, as though they would say ' Un-
harness us.   It can't be done.'   The
drivers on these roads, who certainly get
over the ground in a manner which is quite
miraculous, so twist and turn the team
about in forcing a passage, corkscrew fashion, through the bogs and swamps, that it
was quite a common circumstance on looking out of the window, to see the coachman
with the ends of a pair of reins in his
hands, apparently driving nothing, or play-
ing at horses, and the leaders staring at
one unexpectedly from the back of the
coach, as if they had some idea of getting
up behind.   A great portion of the way
was over what is called a corduroy road,
which is made by throwing trunks of trees
into a marsh, and leaving them to settle
there.   The very slightest of the jolts with
which the ponderous carriage fell from log
to log, was enough, it seemed, to have dis-
located all the bones in the human body.
It would be impossible to experience a
similar set of sensations, in any other circumstances, unless perhaps in attempting
to go up to the top of St. Paul's in an

omnibus. Never, never once, that day, was the coach in any position, attitude, or kind of motion to which we are accustomed in coaches. Never did it make the smallest approach to one's experience of the proceedings of any sort of vehicle that goes on wheels.

" Still, it was a fine day, and the temperature was delicious, and though we had left Summer behind us in the west, and were fast leaving Spring, we were moving towards Niagara and home. We alighted in a pleasant wood towards the middle of the day, dined on a fallen tree, and leaving our best fragments with a cottager, and our worst with the pigs (who swarm in this part of the country like grains of sand on the sea-shore, to the great comfort of our commissariat in Canada), we went forward again, gaily.

" As night came on, the track grew narrower and narrower, until at last it so lost itself among the trees, that the driver seemed to find his way by instinct. We had the comfort of knowing, at least, that there was no danger of his falling asleep, for every now and then a wheel would strike against an unseen stump with such a jerk, that he was fain to hold on pretty tight and pretty quick to keep himself upon the box. Nor was there any reason to dread the least danger from furious driving, inasmuch as over that broken ground the horses had enough to do to walk; as to shying, there was no room for that; and a herd of wild elephants could not have run away in such a wood, with such a coach at their heels. So we stumbled along, quite satisfied.

"These stumps of trees are a curious feature in American travelling. The varying illusions they present to the unaccustomed eye as it grows dark, are quite astonishing in their number and reality. Now, there is a Grecian urn erected in the centre of a lonely field; now there is a woman weeping at a tomb; now a very comonplace old gentleman in a white waist-coat, with a thumb thrust into each arm-hole of his coat; now a student poring on a book; now a crouching negro; now, a horse, a dog, a cannon, an armed man; a hunch-back throwing off his cloak and stepping forth into the light. They were often as entertaining to me as so many glasses in

a magic lantern, and never took their
shapes at my bidding, but seemed to force
themselves upon me, whether I would or
no: and strange to say, I sometimes
recognized in them counterparts of figures
once familiar to me in pictures attached to
childish books, forgotten long ago.

" It soon became too dark, however, even
for this amusement, and the trees were so
close together that their dry branches rattled against the coach on either side, and
obliged us all to keep our heads within. It
lightened too, for three whole hours; each
flash being very bright, and blue, and long;
and as the vivid streaks came darting in
among the crowded branches, and the
thunder rolled gloomily above the tree tops,
one could scarcely help thinking that there
were better neighbourhoods at such a time
than thick woods afforded.

" At length, between ten and eleven
o'clock at night, a few feeble lights appeared in the distance, and Upper Sandusky, an Indian village, where we were to
stay till morning, lay before us."

Dickens's description of his visit to
" Looking-Glass Prairie " from St. Louis is

full of amusement, and contains many
vivid pictures of pioneer roads and taverns
in the Mississippi Valley:

" As I had a great desire to see a Prairie
before turning back from the furthest point
of my wanderings; and as some gentlemen
of the town had, in their hospitable consideration, an equal desire to gratify me;
a day was fixed, before my departure, for an
expedition to the Looking-Glass Prairie,
which is within thirty miles of the town.
Deeming it possible that my readers may
not object to know what kind of thing such
a gipsy party may be at that distance from
home, and among what sort of objects it
moves, I will describe the jaunt.　.　.

" I may premise that the word Prairie is
variously pronounced *paraaer*, *parearer*, and
paroarer. The latter mode of pronunciation is perhaps the most in favour. We
were fourteen in all, and all young men:
indeed it is a singular though very natural
feature in the society of these distant settlements, that it is mainly composed of adven-
turous persons in the prime of life, and has
very few grey heads among it. There
were no ladies: the trip being a fatiguing

one: and we were to start at five o'clock in the morning punctually.   .   .

"At seven o'clock .   . the party had assembled, and were gathered round one light carriage, with a very stout axle-tree; one something on wheels like an amateur carrier's cart; one double phaeton of great antiquity and unearthly construction; one gig with a great hole in its back and a broken head; and one rider on horse-back who was to go on before. I got into the first coach with three companions; the rest bestowed themselves in the other vehicles; two large baskets were made fast to the lightest; two large stone jars in wicker cases, technically known as demi-johns, were consigned to the 'least rowdy' of the party for safe keeping; and the procession moved off to the ferry-boat, in which it was to cross the river bodily, men, horses, carriages, and all as the manner in these parts is.

"We got over the river in due course, and mustered again before a little wooden box on wheels, hove down all aslant in a morass, with 'MERCHANT TAILOR' painted in very large letters over the door. Hav-

ing settled the order of proceeding, and the
road to be taken, we started off once more
and began to make our way through an
ill-favoured Black Hollow, called, less
expressively, the American Bottom.   .   .

" We had a pair of very strong horses,
but travelled at the rate of little more than
a couple of miles an hour, through one
unbroken slough of black mud and water.
It had no variety but in depth. Now it
was only half over the wheels, now it hid
the axletree, and now the coach sank down
in it almost to the windows. The air re-
sounded in all directions with the loud
chirping of the frogs, who, with the pigs
(a coarse, ugly breed, as unwholesome-look-
ing as though they were the spontaneous
growth of the country), had the whole
scene to themselves. Here and there we
passed a log hut; but the wretched cabins
were wide apart and thinly scattered, for
though the soil is very rich in this place,
few people can exist in such a deadly
atmosphere. On either side of the track,
if it deserve the name, was the thick
' bush;' and everywhere was stagnant,
slimy, rotten, filthy water.

" As it is the custom in these parts to
give a horse a gallon or so of cold water
whenever he is in a foam with heat, we
halted for that purpose, at a log inn in the
wood, far removed from any other residence. It consisted of one room, bare-
roofed and bare-walled of course, with a
loft above. The ministering priest was a
swarthy young savage, in a shirt of cotton
print like bed-furniture, and a pair of
ragged trousers. There were a couple of
young boys, too, nearly naked, lying idly
by the well; and they, and he, and *the*
traveller at the inn, turned out to look
at us.   .   .

" When the horses were swollen out to
about twice their natural dimensions (there
seems to be an idea here, that this kind of
inflation improves their going), we went
forward again, through mud and mire, and
damp, and festering heat, and brake and
bush, attended always by the music of the
frogs and pigs, until nearly noon, when we
halted at a place called Belleville.

" Belleville was a small collection of
wooden houses, huddled together in the
very heart of the bush and swamp.   .   .

The criminal court was sitting, and was at that moment trying some criminals for horse-stealing; with whom it would most likely go hard: for live stock of all kinds being necessarily very much exposed in the woods, is held by the community in rather higher value than human life; and for this reason, juries generally make a point of finding all men indicted for cattle-stealing, guilty, whether or no. The horses belonging to the bar, the judge, and witnesses, were tied to temporary racks set up roughly in the road; by which is to be understood, a forest path, nearly knee-deep in mud and slime.

" There was an hotel in this place which, like all hotels in America, had its large dining-room for the public table. It was an odd, shambling, low-roofed out-house, half cowshed and half kitchen, with a coarse brown canvas table-cloth, and tin sconces stuck against the walls, to hold candles at supper-time. The horseman had gone forward to have coffee and some eatables prepared, and they were by this time nearly ready. He had ordered ' wheat-bread and chicken fixings,' in preference to

'corn-bread and common doings.'[47] The latter kind of refection includes only pork and
bacon. The former comprehends broiled
ham, sausages, veal cutlets, steaks, and
such other viands of that nature as may be
supposed, by a tolerably wide poetical construction, ' to fix' a chicken comfortably
in the digestive organs of any lady or gentleman.   .   .

" From Belleville, we went on, through
the same desolate kind of waste, and constantly attended, without the interval of a
moment, by the same music; until, at
three o'clock in the afternoon, we halted
once more at a village called Lebanon to
inflate the horses again, and give them
some corn besides: of which they stood
much in need. Pending this ceremony, I
walked into the village, where I met a full
sized dwelling-house coming down-hill at
a round trot, drawn by a score or more of
oxen. The public-house was so very clean
and good a one, that the managers of the
jaunt resolved to return to it and put up
there for the night, if possible. This

[47] See *Historic Highways of America*, vol. xi, p.
199, *note*.

course decided on, and the horses being well refreshed, we again pushed forward, and came upon the Prairie at sunset.

" It would be difficult to say why, or how — though it was possibly from having heard and read so much about it — but the effect on me was disappointment. Looking towards the setting sun, there lay, stretched out before my view, a vast expanse of level ground; unbroken, save by one thin line of trees, which scarcely amounted to a scratch upon the great blank; until it met the glowing sky, wherein it seemed to dip: mingling with its rich colours, and mellowing in its distant blue. There it lay, a tranquil sea or lake without water, if such a simile be admissible, with the day going down upon it; a few birds wheeling here and there; and solitude and silence reigning paramount around. But the grass was not yet high; there were bare black patches on the ground; and the few wild flowers that the eye could see, were poor and scanty. Great as the picture was, its very flatness and extent, which left nothing to the imagination, tamed it down and cramped

its interest. I felt little of that sense of
freedom and exhilaration which a Scottish
heath inspires, or even our English downs
awaken. It was lonely and wild, but op-
pressive in its barren monotony. I felt
that in traversing the Prairies, I could
never abandon myself to the scene, forget-
ful of all else; as I should do instinctively,
were the heather underneath my feet, or an
iron-bound coast beyond; but should often
glance towards the distant and frequently-
receding line of the horizon, and wish it
gained and passed. It is not a scene to be
forgotten, but it is scarcely one, I think
(at all events, as I saw it), to remember with
much pleasure, or to covet the looking-on
again, in after life.

" We encamped near a solitary log-house,
for the sake of its water, and dined upon
the plain. The baskets contained roast
fowls, buffalo's tongue (an exquisite dainty,
by the way), ham, bread, cheese, and butter; biscuits, champagne, sherry; lemons
and sugar for punch; and abundance of
rough ice. The meal was delicious, and
the entertainers were the soul of kindness
and good humour. I have often recalled

that cheerful party to my pleasant recollection since, and shall not easily forget, in junketings nearer home with friends of older date, my boon companions on the Prairie. Returning to Lebanon that night, we lay at the little inn at which we had halted in the afternoon. In point of cleanliness and comfort it would have suffered by no comparison with any village alehouse, of a homely kind, in England. . .

" After breakfast, we started to return by a different way from that which we had taken yesterday, and coming up at ten o'clock with an encampment of German emigrants carrying their goods in carts, who had made a rousing fire which they were just quitting, we stopped there to refresh. And very pleasant the fire was; for, hot though it had been yesterday, it was quite cold to-day, and the wind blew keenly. Looming in the distance, as we rode along, was another of the ancient Indian burial-places, called The Monks' Mound; in memory of a body of fanatics of the order of La Trappe, who founded a desolate convent there, many years ago, when there were no settlers within a thou-

sand miles, and were all swept off by the
pernicious climate: in which lamentable
fatality, few rational people will suppose,
perhaps, that society experienced any very
severe deprivation.

" The track of to-day had the same features as the track of yesterday. There
was the swamp, the bush, the perpetual
chorus of frogs, the rank unseemly growth,
the unwholesome steaming earth. Here
and there, and frequently too, we encountered a solitary broken-down waggon, full
of some new settler's goods. It was a
pitiful sight to see one of these vehicles
deep in the mire; the axletree broken; the
wheel lying idly by its side; the man gone
miles away, to look for assistance; the
woman seated among their wandering
household gods with a baby at her breast,
a picture of forlorn, dejected patience; the
team of oxen crouching down mournfully
in the mud, and breathing forth such clouds
of vapour from their mouths and nostrils,
that all the damp mist and fog around
seemed to have come direct from them.

" In due time we mustered once again
before the merchant tailor's, and having

done so, crossed over to the city in the ferry-boat: passing, on the way, a spot called Bloody Island, the duelling-ground of St. Louis, and so designated in honour of the last fatal combat fought there, which was with pistols, breast to breast. Both combatants fell dead upon the ground; and possibly some rational people may think of them, as of the gloomy madmen on the Monks' Mound, that they were no great loss to the community."

For purposes of comparison, the following description of experiences in later times with Indian trails of the West will be of interest. Much that has been deduced from a study of our pioneer history and embodied in the preceding pages finds strong confirmation here; in earlier days, with forests covering the country, the trails were more like roads than in the open prairies of the West; but, as will be seen, many laws governed the earlier and the later Indian thoroughfares, alike. I quote from the Hon. Charles Augustus Murray's memoirs, written three-quarters of a century ago, of a tour in Missouri:

" On the 18th we pursued our course,
north by east: this was not exactly the
direction in which I wished to travel, but
two considerations induced me to adopt it
at this part of the journey. In the first
place, it enabled me to keep along the
dividing ridge; an advantage so great, and
so well understood by all prairie travellers,
that it is worth making a circuit of several
miles a day to keep it; and the Indian
trails which we have crossed since our
residence in the wilderness, convince me
that the savages pay the greatest attention
to this matter. In a wide extent of country composed of a succession of hills and
ridges, it is evident there must be a great
number of steep banks, which offer to an
inexperienced traveller numerous obstacles,
rendering his own progress most toilsome,
and that of loaded packhorses almost
impossible. If these ridges all ran in
parallel lines, and were regular in their
formation, nothing would be more simple
than to get upon the summit of one, and
keep it for the whole day's journey: but
such is not the case; they constantly meet
other ridges running in a transverse direc-

tion; and, of course, large dips and ravines
are consequent upon that meeting. The
' dividing ridge ' of a district is that which,
while it is, as it were, the back-bone of the
range of which it forms a part, heads at
the same time all the transverse ravines,
whether on the right or on the left hand,
and thereby spares to the traveller an
infinity of toilsome ascent and descent.

" I have sometimes observed that an
Indian trail wound through a country in a
course perfectly serpentine, and appeared
to me to travel three miles when only one
was necessary. It was not till my own
practical experience had made me attend
more closely to this matter, that I learnt to
appreciate its importance. I think that
the first quality in a guide through an
unknown range of rolling prairie, is having
a good and a quick eye for hitting off the
' dividing ridge; ' the second, perhaps, in
a western wilderness, is a ready and almost
intuitive perception (so often found in an
Indian) of the general character of a country, so as to be able to bring his party to
water when it is very scarce.   .   .

A few miles farther we crossed an old

Indian trail I think it was of a Pawnee
party, for it bore north by west .   . it
had not been a war-party, as was evident
from the character of the trail. A war-
party leaves only the trail of the horses, or,
of course, if it be a foot party, the still
slighter tracks of their own feet; but when
they are on their summer hunt, or migrat-
ing from one region to another, they take
their squaws and children with them, and
this trail can always be distinguished from
the former, by two parallel tracks about
three and a half feet apart, not unlike
those of a light pair of wheels: these are
made by the points of the long curved
poles on which their lodges are stretched,
the thickest or butt ends of which are
fastened to each side of the pack-saddle,
while the points trail behind the horse; in
crossing rough or boggy places, this is
often found the most inconvenient part of
an Indian camp equipage. .   . I was
fortunate enough to find an Indian trail
bearing north by east, which was *s near
to our destined course as these odious
creeks would permit us to go. We struck
into it, and it brought us safely, though

not without difficulty, through the tangled
and muddy bottom in which we had been
involved: sometimes a horse floundered,
and more than once a pack came off; but
upon the whole we had great reason to
congratulate ourselves upon having found
this trail, by which we escaped in two
hours from a place which would, without
its assistance, probably have detained us
two days. I was by no means anxious to
part with so good a friend, and proceeded
some miles upon this same trail; it was
very old and indistinct, especially in the
high and dry parts of the prairie. I left
my horse with the rest of the party and
went on foot, in order that I might more
easily follow the trail, which became almost
imperceptible as we reached an elevated
district of table-land, which had been
burned so close that I very often lost the
track altogether for fifty yards. If a fire
takes place on a prairie where there is
already a distinct trail, it is as easy to follow it, if not more so than before; because
the short and beaten grass offering no food
to the fire, partly escapes its fury, and
remains a green line upon a sea of black;

but if the party making the trail pass
over a prairie which is already burnt, in
the succeeding season when the new grass
has grown, it can scarcely be traced by any
eye but that of an Indian.   .   . After
we had travelled five hours .   . I
found that the trail which we had been
following, merged in another and a larger
one, which appeared to run a point to the
west of north. This was so far out of our
course that I hesitated whether I should
not leave it altogether; but, upon reflec-
tion, I determined not to do so .   . if
I attempted to cross the country farther to
the eastward, without any trail, I should
meet with serious difficulties and delays.   .   . I therefore struck into it,
and ere long the result justified my con-
jecture; for we came to a wooded bottom
or valley, which was such a complete jun-
gle, and so extensive, that I am sure, if we
had not been guided by the trail, we could
not have made our way through it in a
week. As it was, the task was no easy
one; for the trail, though originally large,
was not very fresh, and the weeds and
branches had in many places so overgrown

it, that I was obliged to dismount and trace it out on foot. It wound about with a hundred serpentine evolutions to avoid the heavy swamps and marshes around us; and I repeatedly thought that, if we lost it, we never should extricate our baggage: even with its assistance, we were obliged frequently to halt and replace the packs, which were violently forced off by the branches with which they constantly came in contact . . 'where on earth is he taking us now? — why we are going back in the same direction as we came!' I turned round and asked the speaker (a comrade) . . to point with his finger to the quarter which he would make for if he were guiding the party to Fort Leavenworth. He did so; and I took out my compass and showed him that he was pointing south-west, *i.e.* to Santa Fé and the Gulf of California: so completely had the poor fellow's head become puzzled by the winding circuit we had made in the swamp." [48]

[48] *Travels in North America* (London, 1839), vol. ii, pp. 29-48.

Important
Historical Publications
OF
The Arthur H. Clark Company

Full descriptive circulars will be mailed
on application

The Philippine Islands
1493 - 1898

Being the history of the Philippines
from their discovery to the present time

EXPLORATIONS by early Navigators, descriptions of the Islands and their Peoples, their History, and records of the Catholic Missions, as related in
contemporaneous books and manuscripts, showing the
political, economic, commercial, and religious conditions of those Islands from their earliest relations with
European Nations to the end of the nineteenth century.

Translated, and edited and annotated by E. H. BLAIR, *and*
J. A. ROBERTSON, *with introduction and additional notes
by* E. G. BOURNE.

With Analytical Index and Illustrations. Limited edition, fifty-five volumes, large 8vo, cloth, uncut, gilt top.
Price, $4.00 net per volume.

Early Western Travels
1748-1846

A SERIES OF ANNOTATED REPRINTS of some of the best and rarest contemporary volumes of travel, descriptive of the Aborigines and Social and Economic Conditions in the Middle and Far West, during the Period of Early American Settlement.

Edited, with Historical, Geographical, Ethnological, and Bibliographical Notes, and Introductions and Index, by

Reuben Gold Thwaites

Editor of "The Jesuit Relations and Allied Documents," "Wisconsin Historical Collections," "Chronicles of Border Warfare," "Hennepin's New Discovery," etc.

With facsimiles of the original title-pages, maps, portraits, views, etc. 31 volumes, large 8vo, cloth, uncut, gilt tops. Price $4.00 net per volume (except the Maximilien Atlas, which is $15.00 net). Limited edition; each set numbered and signed.

An Elaborate Analytical Index to the Whole
Almost all of the rare originals are without indexes. In the present reprint series, this immense mass of historical data will be made accessible through one exhaustive analytical index, to occupy the concluding volume.

Mr. Thwaites's Eminence as an authority on all matters connected with the history of the West, and his well-known standing as an Editor and Librarian, will be sufficient assurance of the value of the Travels selected, and of the care with which the series will be edited throughout.